What people are

Taking

It is our personal relationships that define our humanity, and the things at which we stumble, the questions with which we grapple, provide the moments of encounter, of discovery. Fiona Gardner draws upon her insights as a theologian and a psychotherapist to point us towards the God who gives shape and meaning to our inner journey.
John Moses, Dean Emeritus of St Paul's London and author of *The Art of Thomas Merton* and *Divine Discontent.*

There is nothing more personal than one's spiritual journey. And yet, it is precisely the particularity of our quest for transcendence that makes the lessons learned and relationships built along the way universally recognizable and relatable. Fiona Gardner shares with us the journeys of four seekers, each with their own joys and hopes, challenges and anxieties, but each illuminating a path to the spiritual through the heart. This book is more than an introduction to the spiritual life; it is a compass pointing the way for modern women and men searching for a profounder sense of spirituality and a deeper sense of self!
Daniel P. Horan, OFM and author, *All God's Creatures: A Theology of Creation, The Franciscan Heart of Thomas Merton* and *Dating God.*

Everyone, knowingly or not, is on a life-path towards wisdom and spiritual maturity. An insightful guide for the journey, Fiona Gardner knows God dwells in our hearts and shows us reliably here how to find Him – a heart-warming read.
Larry Culliford, author of *Much Ado about Something* and *The Big Book of Wisdom.*

Taking Heart

Four accounts of spiritual searching,
self-acceptance and journeying to the
heart of faith

Taking Heart

Four accounts of spiritual searching,
self-acceptance and journeying to the
heart of faith

Fiona Gardner

CHRISTIAN ALTERNATIVE
BOOKS

Winchester, UK
Washington, USA

JOHN HUNT PUBLISHING

First published by Christian Alternative Books, 2021
Christian Alternative Books is an imprint of John Hunt Publishing Ltd.,
No. 3 East St., Alresford, Hampshire SO24 9EE, UK
office@jhpbooks.com
www.johnhuntpublishing.com
www.christian-alternative.com

For distributor details and how to order please visit the 'Ordering' section on our website.

ISBN: 978 1 78904 543 7
978 1 78904 544 4 (ebook)
Library of Congress Control Number: 2019956112

A CIP catalogue record for this book is available from the British Library.

Design: Stuart Davies

UK: Printed and bound by CPI Group (UK) Ltd, Croydon, CR0 4YY
US: Printed and bound by Thomson-Shore, 7300 West Joy Road, Dexter, MI 48130

We operate a distinctive and ethical publishing philosophy in all areas of our business, from our global network of authors to production and worldwide distribution.

Contents

The Only Mind Worth Having, Thomas Merton and the Child Mind, (2015) Eugene, Oregon: Cascade Books. ISBN 13: 978–1–4982–3022–3

Precious Thoughts, Daily Readings from the Correspondence of Thomas Merton, (2011) London: Darton, Longman and Todd. ISBN: 978–0–232–52883–1

Researching, Reflecting and Writing about Work, Co-edited with Steven J. Coombs, (2010) London: Routledge. ISBN: 978–0–415–47230–2

The Four Steps of Love, (2007) London: Darton, Longman and Todd. ISBN: –13 978–0–232–52716–2

Journeying Home, (2004) London: Darton, Longman and Todd. ISBN: 0 232 52524 2

Self-Harm: A Psychotherapeutic Approach, (2001) London and New York: Brunner Routledge ISBN: 0–415–23303–8

For Hugh Gee

There is within each of us a secret place, the inner chamber of our hearts, a place so secret that not only is it hidden from the world outside us, it is not even fully known to ourselves ... It is the place where God hides himself ... here we can touch the hem of God's garment. **Alexander Ryrie**

Preface

I know and have seen what I was obscurely looking for.[1]

These words are part of the description given by Thomas Merton when he stood in front of the large Buddhist statues in Polonnaruwa, in what is now Sri Lanka, and I quote them again at the end of this book. When I first read the account of Merton's epiphany I found it electrifying. As the Quaker George Fox might have said, "it really spoke to my condition." For many years I had been spiritually searching and by the end of the 1990s I was spiritually in limbo. I had been a Quaker, a member of The Society of Friends, for about twenty years; but had begun to feel that something was missing. At the same time, I had experimented with different Buddhist groups, was seriously involved in yoga and had traveled to India in search of "enlightenment" – but returned ill. At that point I stopped attending Quaker meeting and let go of the searching. It didn't seem possible to find whatever it was I was looking for.

In the early 1990s, as part of my obscure looking, I had read a second-hand copy of *The Seven Storey Mountain*, the early autobiography written by Thomas Merton, and had felt absorbed by the narrative, identifying in many ways with Merton's early life; but the fervor of his conversion and subsequent arrival at the Abbey of Gethsemani to become a Trappist monk had felt only something I could imagine. However, in 1999 I fell over, literally, *The Other Side of the Mountain*, which was volume seven, the last of the journals of Thomas Merton that ended with his death in 1968. Some copies had been stacked on the floor of the local bookshop, rather symbolically I later thought, between the religion and psychology sections (as I was then working as a psychotherapist), and as I picked myself up I also picked up one which I then bought. The cover helped, it seemed as if Thomas

1

Merton was smiling and encouraging me to have a look inside, he also looked fun. Here was someone, a person I already knew a bit about, now writing about a journey to India, so perhaps he could help.

After reading that volume I was hooked and so read one by one, working randomly in no particular order through each of the earlier *Journals* and loved them. However, this was not just a literary venture: it became transformational. I now realize that this reading was a form of preparation for my own conversion, and that in some way my mind was becoming open to welcome a deeper experience of God and a sense of personal relationship with Jesus Christ. Everything changed, I got confirmed and late in 2001, I went on a day retreat about Thomas Merton, and then joined The Thomas Merton Society of Great Britain and Ireland and later the International Thomas Merton Society. The first residential conference I attended I found inspirational, a community of like-minded people. In part, as a way of expressing my gratitude for the transformation that was effected in my life through reading Merton, I have been involved in promoting his work and spiritual experiences ever since, for a while chairing the Society and later editing the *Merton Journal*. In 2015 I was awarded a Louie by the International Thomas Merton Society for my work on Merton. I am now a spiritual director, on the front line of spiritual searching, a searching that of course continues throughout our life.

It was Merton who said that God puts into our hands the books that we might need to read, and, so, this book is offered in that same spirit to all who might be searching and journeying to the heart of faith.

Foreword

In the last few centuries, the mind has come up in the world, the heart demoted. It's a reordering that has not served us well. Hearts of flesh have become hearts of stone. The demotion of the heart helps explain why so many of us feel lost in the cosmos with little if any sense of ultimate meaning or the creator's presence. As David Bentley Hart has written in *The Experience of God*: "Somehow, we have as a culture forgotten being: the self-evident mystery of existence … Human beings have never before lived lives so remote from nature, or been so insensible to the enigma it embodies. For late modern peoples God has become ever more a myth …"

The heart is not only a blood-pumping muscle but represents the core of our identity, the ground zero of communion with God, the center point of love, the core of compassion, the home base of the soul, the domain of prayer and conscience. If we wish to be well in soul as well as body, we need to pay more attention to our hearts.

Few of us would claim to have untroubled, unwounded hearts. At least some of the time, we're all dealing with old resentments, unhealed wounds, bitter memories, words we wish we hadn't said and acts we wish we hadn't done. We all have damaged hearts.

This small book is about the healing of the heart. Its author, Fiona Gardner, could be described as a spiritual cardiologist. Her professional background is as a psychoanalytic psychotherapist. Though no longer in practice as a therapist, she has become a spiritual director. In *Taking Heart*, she writes not only about theory and theology, but her experiences as a guide to four of the people – Carly, Frank, Helen and Stuart – who have sought her help.

What sort of help and with what results? You are about to

3

find out.

Jim Forest

Author of *Writing Straight with Crooked Lines: A Memoir, The Root of War Is Fear: Thomas Merton's Advice to Peacemakers,* and *Loving Our Enemies: Reflections on the Hardest Commandment.*

Acknowledgments

I would like to thank all those with whom I've worked in spiritual direction over the past ten years and especially to those who have contributed to this book. Appreciation also goes to those who have spiritually influenced me at church, through friendship, on retreat, in discussion and through their writings.

I am especially grateful to Jim Forest for his foreword, and to John Moses, Dan Horan and Larry Culliford who have endorsed the book.

Thanks to the team at John Hunt Publishing for their professionalism.

As always, loving thanks goes to Peter Ellis for his help and support.

Finally, this book is dedicated with thanks to Hugh Gee, psyche-analyst, for his psychological and spiritual insights over the years.

Introduction

> I will give them a heart to know that I am the Lord; and they shall be my people and I will be their God, for they shall return to me with their whole heart. *Jeremiah 24: 7*

One of the central tenets of this book is that spiritual life is always personal, and the deeper the spiritual life is, the more personal it becomes. Religious worship and shared spiritual practices can provide an outer home, a framework and a sense of community and companionship, but the meaning and the mystery is ultimately found in a deeply private and personal meaningful relationship in our heart of hearts – sometimes with another and sometimes found alone with God. In this book the experiences of four people who are spiritually searching are explored, and their different journeys through self-doubt to self-acceptance and to the heart of faith are discussed. The four: Carly, Frank, Helen and Stuart are not especially religious or spiritual and nor are they famous – you might even use the word "ordinary" to describe them – yet all four are on an "extraordinary" search for meaning.

The meaning that they are searching for is God. God can be found on the surface and he can be denied on the surface, but it is only on the surface level of life that God can be ignored or denied. Once any of us go below the surface level we come up against the crucial questions because at some point or another, and, often when things are going badly wrong, everyone yearns to find meaning and a sense of what life is about. The questions we ask are those that ultimately lie at the heart of each person: What is the meaning of life? Can any explanations answer that? Why is there evil? What might it mean to live a good life? Who am I really? Why has this happened to me? As we search for answers and seek for truth often in the face of apparent absurdity, the commonplace, the trivial and the one-dimensional falls away, a door opens to the deeper level, and our human experience is confronted by something more than ourselves which some call God. Sometimes the events that surround us feel impossible – unbearable. After all, as has been said, we can only take so much of reality at any one time. And yet within ourselves, deep in our hearts, lies the door to the profound levels of reality that give us the only possible approach to meaningful existence itself.

The searcher, or the searching part of our selves, appears out of the apparent randomness of all the various events and circumstances that make up each of our "ordinary" lives. This includes the good things and the not so good and the downright bad. It also includes all the mistakes and contradictions, the successes and the imperfections, the pleasures and the frustrations and anger, the criticism of others and the self-criticism, love and the loss of love and the turning of love into hate; all the connections and the separations, and the myriad of emotions and happenings are all expressions of the same life force, and contribute to the sense of who each one of us is. While it is usually difficult to accept all these different parts of ourselves, through the accounts given by the four whose spiritual journeys are described, we can see that self-acceptance lies at the heart of genuine faith. This book is then about coming to understand that it is in our heart of hearts that we find a direct experience of God. The search is for a profound and inner hope of the reality of the living God, and for an experience that deepens and feeds faith in the depths of our hearts.

The heart symbolizes the taproot of our being. It is the place where we find meaning and from which our deepest self operates. The heart is the place where our full intellect, our will and devotion, and our emotions and feelings connect and interweave; it is the center of being alive both physically and spiritually. The word "heart" both in everyday language and in the spiritual and religious contexts is one of those words which generate other words and some of these are difficult to define and often full of meaning. The word heart is highly evocative, for every one of us has a heart that keeps us alive. But the word is also powerful, and communicates a deep and complex reality because it can act as a descriptor for who we are. While it is a physical truth that each one of us has a heart, it may not mean that we are capable of love; that we are able to be warm and affectionate. Our hearts can be empty or full, soft or hardened, and it may take time for our personal identity to develop as we encounter one another in the world. As self-conscious beings, we see that the symbol of the heart acts as a container for all the diverse experiences and interactions in our lives; the locus for both integration and disintegration.

We live in a time when we differentiate between head and heart; where head is seen as the container for reason, for rational, sensible and decisive thinking. As craniological twenty-first-century beings we are tuned into current preoccupations with logic, pragmatism, science, technology and economy. Yet our beating heart is a bodily reminder of the connection between mind and body, we physically react to what we are feeling. We understand the heart as symbolizing the passionate, the intuitive and sometimes the irrational, it is seen as the feeling and emotional part of ourselves. We speak of the battle between head and heart as if one of them has to win, where the struggle seems to be between knowing what the brain and mind are telling us, or, listening to what our heart is feeling and saying. If we are described as being led by the heart, then the implication is that intellect and thinking is pushed aside for feelings; one of the ideas in this book is that both have to be held in balance, in a tension of what appears to be opposites.

The heart is also of course a universal symbol symbolizing love in a way that the brain and the mind cannot. The iconic image is of the two halves balanced and between them an indentation – and as so is aesthetically pleasing. This symbol of love implying emotion and affections can also be expanded further to authenticity, courage, kindness and goodness. It is seen as an essence of our inner self. As a container for love, the heart is also recognized as fragile and breakable; unrequited or unhappy love leads to a broken-heart. Our sincerity is seen as coming from "our heart of hearts," where we "speak from the bottom of our heart"; and such speaking can include worry and concern so that "one's heart goes out to someone" or "we take something to heart." We can "take heart" or "lose heart," "not have the heart to do something" or a "sinking heart." Our hearts might be "a heart of gold" or "of stone"; we can be "big-hearted" or at the other extreme "we can have no heart at all," be "warm-hearted" or "cold-hearted." We can "learn something by heart" or have "a change of heart," and we can "set our hearts on fire," while the "heart of the matter" is the center or core of something.

In the context of religion and spirituality we are taken deeper beyond the more superficial interpretation of the level of feelings associated with the sentimental and the erotic, for here something more is included. In the Judeo-Christian tradition, the symbol of the heart certainly implies the depths beyond surface ritual and concerns; it points towards a turning to meaning, purpose, truth and the inner world, and a further implication is about *being itself,* and towards what the true self might be. It can offer a deeper and different way of thinking, beyond the merely factual or precise. It is the focal center of our personhood, the deepest psychological ground of our personality which is created in the image and likeness of God. As the monk and writer Thomas Merton puts it, the heart is "the root and source of all one's own inner truth."[1] As a symbol, it gives us space for our imagination, and for our soul and mind to expand. As Christians, we are asked to love God with all of our heart, and to open our hearts to God who knows all the secrets that are hidden there.

Yet as with the two halves of the heart, there is also the shadow aspect of the positive characteristics of love, passion, authenticity and goodness – hate, indifference, falsity and things that are not good. As the fourth-century Orthodox mystic Makarios the Great describes it there are all things in the heart. He writes of "unfathomable depths":

Within the heart... there are reception rooms and bedchambers in it, doors and porches, and many offices and passages. In it is the workshop of righteousness and of wickedness. In it is death; in it is life ... The heart is Christ's palace; there Christ the King comes to take his rest, with the angels and spirits of the saints, and he dwells there, walking within it and placing his Kingdom there.[2]

Theophan the Recluse, an Orthodox saint, also saw the heart as the location for self-awareness and the innermost spirit of a person. He wrote that here was included conscience, the idea of God, and the nature of the relationship with God, and "all the treasures of the spiritual life." In other words, the heart clearly represents the core of being and the soul, and part of our life journey is for us to know what we are feeling in our heart so as to create a space there for the indwelling of God. The heart is the space where we meet God, and "where transcendence and immanence meet in unity." This means that the essence of spiritual life is to metaphorically open the heart to God, and, to try to keep it open. In a similar way, other religious traditions also point to the heart as the place to meet God. In Islamic mystical traditions Mohammed, in a central teaching, is quoted as saying that: "The heart of the believer is the place of the revelation of God ... the throne of God ... the mirror of God." The Quran states that it is only by listening and witnessing that the spiritual heart is awakened and transformed; otherwise the heart becomes deadened, blind or hardened. Whilst the mystic Sufi poet Rumi tells us that the mirror of the heart is limitless but nevertheless that as you live deeper in the heart, the mirror gets clearer and cleaner! It is in the heart we find our self and we find God: "for the Heart is with God or rather the Heart is God." In the Hindu and Buddhist Chakra way of envisaging, the heart-center is called the Anahata, and is the center where we can know direct connection with the divine. It is in the "cave of the heart" that the entire universe is said to be contained, alive and blazing in divine light, and is the site of ultimate divine realization.

All spiritual journeys are journeys of the heart, and like the two halves of the heart include many mixed experiences and feelings: surface and depth, the good and the bad, the person we present to the world and the shadow part of ourselves that we would prefer to keep hidden. The journey is above all about moving from a predominantly closed heart, dominated by self-love and self-doubt, and where temptations and distractions obscure the truth for us, to a heart that is predominantly accepting of all parts of ourselves, and having nothing to hide is open to God and to love – indeed to the love of God. The open heart is not one sided, but rather allows all the experiences to be held in balance, holding all opposing emotions in a state of awareness of the ground of our being.

In this book the accounts of four people participating in a journey of the heart, a journey in search of God and of themselves are described; they shared their experiences with me over many years and are happy to share them now with you. As with all journeys there is discovering, but also an uncovering and a recovering; although their experiences are contextually different, they are all connected through the divine presence. All heart journeys are an exodus that take us out of captivity in some form or other, and are also the passion story which is at the heart of the mystery of faith, a journey through the very worst and towards the very best. And throughout the spiritual journey, God is shaping and forming our inner life in the unknown depths of our heart.

Chapter 1

Hungry Hearts – Seeking God in the Wilderness

There was no direction in which I could bring the whole of me completely to bear and I felt rather lonely."[1]

"For surely I know the plans I have for you," says the LORD, "plans for your welfare and not for harm, to give you a future with hope. Then when you call upon me and come and pray to me, I will hear you. When you search for me, you will find me; if you seek me with all your heart." *Jeremiah 29:11–13*

This extract from Jeremiah is part of the story of exile – a state of captivity where we are in exile from the homeland, from the truth and heart of our self and from the heart of God. Exile does not have to be physical and geographical; it can be emotional and spiritual. Harry Williams, priest and author, writes about the urge to evade the responsibility of finding out who we really are; instead we lose or forfeit ourselves – in other words, we exile our heart – the essence of who we are to a far-off place. We find ourselves in a wilderness, a wilderness of inner isolation, where there is an absence of real contact. "It's a sense of being alone – boringly alone, or saddeningly alone, or terrifyingly alone."[2]

We might push this feeling away through denial or by distracting activity, but the cut off, exiled part will always return in one form of another – perhaps in a yearning or searching for something real, something that will touch the heart. We might be someone who already goes to church but feel lost as if a part of us is still looking for something more; we might feel that we are operating under a religious disguise by going through the motions of what is expected rather than really feeling God's presence. Or, we might be someone on the edge of thinking about the spiritual dimension of life, feeling unbalanced because we are living only on the surface. We might perhaps have a realization that our life has been reduced to just being a consumer, and that there has been a depreciation of our spiritual nature – perhaps it feels as if we have lost any sense of enchantment or mystery.

Before his conversion Thomas Merton experienced, "the futile search for satisfaction where it could not be found." He describes his life then as a "blind-alley," whatever he tried as a distraction didn't meet this longing which would not go away, but that "the very anguish and helplessness of my position was something to which I rapidly succumbed. And it was my defeat that was to be the occasion for my rescue."[3] He found that an initial interest in searching for truth opened up further longing, so that his life became one of continual conversion, or we might also use the word discovery. Harry Williams puts it well when he writes, "No, it can be no easy journey, this voyage of discovery in which we set out to find ourselves. The road to the celestial city is a long road."[4] He also saw that although we may think we want to find God, underneath there may be a reluctance to open ourselves to what may be life-changing with all the disruption that that entails.

Often we shall have to allow the dynamite of life to smash up those fixed attitudes of heart and mind which lead us to make demands in their nature self-contradictory. In this sense we shall have often to lose our life in order to find it ...

In her journal, Etty Hillesum, the Dutch author who writes both about her religious awakening and the persecutions of Jewish people in Amsterdam during the German occupation, wrote how:

Everything has gone wrong again. I long for something and

don't know what it is. Inside I am totally at a loss, restless, driven, and my head feels close to bursting again … all the questioning, the discontent, the feeling that everything was empty of meaning, the sense that life was unfulfilled, all that pointless brooding. And right now I am sunk in the mire. And even the certain knowledge that this too will pass has brought me no peace this time.[5]

We might try to find God using our logic or rational reason and thinking, but inside we long for the experience of God's presence: answering the mind's questions is not the same as responding to the heart. For authentic faith that changes our life we cannot be taught or have beliefs imposed on us, instead, and fundamentally, we have to rely on experience and we must not be afraid to trust that experience. True searching is not about the mute God of reason, but about the God of revelation who speaks to the people and to our heart – and that can often be through scripture but also through everyday events and the unexpected.[6]

This is our introduction to Stuart, one of the spiritual seekers whose story is told in this book:

Stuart
I'm getting on a bit, you could call it late middle age or perhaps very late middle age but I'm still searching, and this will sound daft, I'm not really sure what it is I'm searching for. I feel there's something rather than nothing and I know that others have felt whatever it is, as they have a spiritual and religious life … but it has to be said I haven't been able to get hold of whatever *it* is, so basically if there *is* something I want it – and before it's too late. Okay, I'm just going to leap in with this … though it might sound a bit much straightaway: I want to know whether existence is an accident, or whether there is something meaningful about it – perhaps even that it is a blessing and not a misfortune, which is what I often tend

to feel. I don't want just to be resigned, but nor do I want to pretend. There's been suffering in my life, like everyone else, and that's not been nothing, at the time and for a long time after it felt significant. It's definitely been something, and perhaps it's made me a better person ... but for what? I know that's also been true from my work life. I've worked for many years in the housing department, and you see a lot of life there, with all the ups and downs that people go through ... I've often thought there has to be a reason for it all ... yes ... there has to be an explanation, because even if only one child suffered, there has to be meaning – even if animals alone were left to suffer on earth. The current state of the world is not acceptable without some true light on existence, and the meaning of it all.

I think I'm an agnostic ... I have been very doubtful, and affected by all those arguments given out as "scientific" but atheism seems so negative and somehow limiting and short sighted ... what on earth does it mean if there's no hope of finding any meaning for the word "truth" or the distinction of what might be good from what is clearly wrong? Is life worth the trouble of living, because I know it's not just about property or possessions or whatever we're currently persuaded to have? Call me old-fashioned, but I know there's more to it than that, because none of that material stuff holds any meaning when we're up against it ... And, dare I say it ... there is a small part of me still hopeful that before I die the meaning of life will reveal itself.

Stuart's search for meaning is also a search for inner experiencing, a greater interiority in life rather than the surface level of reality. Stuart didn't quote it, but his energy and sincerity brings to mind: "Ask, and you will receive; search and you will find; knock, and the door will be opened for you" (Matthew 7: 7), where the last part of the sentence seems extraordinary: "and the door will be opened *for you*." That is such an invitation – *you only have to knock* and Stuart was certainly knocking. So what wasn't happening? What wasn't he seeing through the open door? Perhaps it's not just Stuart, but in a way we all suffer from blurred vision – for missing the open door. And what if the door was opened, and *is* open, but we can't see through it. As William Blake understood, "If the doors of perception were cleansed everything would appear to man as it is: Infinite."[7] We have, Blake continues, closed ourselves up and only see things through narrow chinks from where we are imprisoned. For when we are offered ordinary reasonableness, good human judgment, scientific facts and common sense they undoubtedly help us to find *some* meaning, but, as the analytical psychologist Carl Jung wrote: "they never take us beyond the frontier of life's most commonplace realities, beyond the merely average and normal."[8] For the knowledge produced in this way is necessarily limited, restricted, and is not able to give us answers to the essential and deeper questions about our existence, about the whole of our life, and about our world. It leaves us in captivity, exiled and limited in our vision.

Stuart continued to explain his seeking by drawing on his spiritual journeying so far:

Stuart

When I was a boy and really right up to my late teens I went to church, but it was primarily a social thing. It was the Methodist church in the small town almost in the very middle of England where I grew up. My parents both went every Sunday, though we never discussed religion at all, then it was just what you did. You dressed in your Sunday best, and I remember my parents shook hands with everyone after and talked about the weather.

There were really good Sunday school classes at the church, which I remember going to for years. What can I take from that? Well a good grounding in Bible stories, and weeks of coloring in maps of Paul's travels all over the place. Then wonders of wonders, when I was about fourteen the church opened a youth group. There were about ten of us, and of course we were all keen to go to that, and it seemed somehow impolite not to keep going to the church too in the morning when they were putting all this on for us in the evening. Now, looking back it was incredibly innocent. We met for a couple of hours at the minister's house, and talked about the social issues of the day and what was happening – there was quite a bit about missionaries I seem to remember. Some Saturday mornings, I think, perhaps only once a month, the group did good works like clearing the gardens of the elderly parishioners or doing some household chores for them, which I remember doing rather badly, but it was a laugh and good fun. It was organized by the minister who we all liked enormously. He was young – well younger than my parents with an attractive smiley wife and a small child, and he was full of energy. I liked the group, because there were girls in it, and as I went to an all-boys school this felt very exciting ... and my good friend Harry came along too.

I think I stopped going to church when I was about eighteen or so, as I moved away to go to University where I found the Christians a dull lot, and there was much better social life going on elsewhere. Perhaps I went again at Christmas, or sometimes when I was home during the holidays, but it felt awkward – almost as if I had let the Methodists down in some way. So, then I didn't go again for years and years.

I think now that I never really thought about what church was, or religion for that matter. The discussions at the youth group were mostly about social action like whether you would fight in a war, or whether we should help people more. Very enjoyable but ... I honestly don't think there was a time then when I wondered whether I actually believed in God or not, and if I did, what that might mean or look like. So, I honestly don't know if I've moved much further on than when I was a teenager, except that now in this the second half of my life, I am full of doubt and questions ... so at least I am curious about it all, whereas then I just took it for granted – so perhaps there is some progress. When we moved here a few years back, my wife was keen that we started to go to church together so that we could get involved and meet people – new people, not just people you see at work every day, so I go every so often to please her really, and once again I'm back with it being mainly a social activity. It's true we've made some good friends, and I'm now on a committee, and volunteer every so often with a social action project that's connected to the church. I like to keep busy, but in terms of my faith or what I believe I just don't know. And more to the point that might be all right if I was happy to leave it like that, but, I feel that somewhere I know there's more to it than that or, if there isn't, I don't want to pretend. Yet no one really talks about their faith, so what do they believe – it can't be what is written in most of the hymns, none of it makes any sense so what is it they know about that I can't seem to? Rosie, that's my wife, says that she feels comforted by going to church, and that she does believe there's a God and that God helps her, but she said talking to me about it made it sound childish, or as if I was questioning or undermining her about it, but that's really the furthest thing from my mind at present. I feel disappointed mostly by the sermons; it's usually about being a nice person and then telling us we should be going out to convince others to come to church – but for what?

There is a contemporary crisis about what we can know, and how we can know about anything in the spiritual realm; what is there in religion that can be proved scientifically, what can be nailed to the laboratory workbench and thoroughly dissected.

As Stuart was conveying, one of the effects of our contemporary way of thinking and seeing the world has been to lose all sense of meaning; a state that leads us to great spiritual impoverishment. Ironically this is a self-created poverty, where imagination and fiction and myth-making is derided or seen as inferior. Our contemporary culture expects direct answers even to the question: "Do you believe that God exists?" so we are expected to answer "yes" or "no" – as if God is an object who exists as you and I exist – and any kind of hedging is regarded suspiciously. Or, the more insidious questioning such as: Why would you believe in God? with the implication that one must be odd, very needy or merely superstitious to do so. The more nuanced approach from previous generations: yes God is a reality, but God cannot be defined, seems now somehow less acceptable. Religion can offer a context to take us beyond the everyday, and so ostensibly it is in church that we might search to find answers to questions about the meaning of life and death, about life's suffering and its profound significance. It is in church that we would hope to find meaning, and meaningful experiences that would offer liberation from the constraints of mere facts. Yet, at your average church service the implication is that we already have the answers, so questions are not raised; the feeling is this is what you do.

What Stuart found was that he was being given apparently the objectivity of truth – this is what is meaningful, and this is what is believed. He found though that the experience was static rather than dynamic – a memory not a movement. What was missing for him was the opening up to the subjective, and to the questioning, to difference and to the spiritual journeying that leads each person to the truth, and the conscience of each person and to the heart of what Stuart earlier called "*it*." The experience of metaphysical anguish, another term for what Stuart expresses, is not new, but for many people in the twenty-first century it is very real, though it may not be recognized as such. This is the despair and desolation at the state of the world and the meaning of existence, and it goes down to the very roots of the desire for life. In the final part of my first meeting with Stuart he ended up saying:

Stuart

So, what do I do? I feel I want and need to do something. I've got fewer years before me now than are behind me, and there's something propelling me to give it a last go to try and find what God is or who God is ... I want to find some meaning in it all, in life and in my life and in what's coming – my death – though hopefully that's still some way away.

Yet I have definitely had meaningful moments, perhaps quite a few, but not in church or to do with religion ... and sometimes in even the dullest of places or in everyday ordinary ways when I have suddenly heard birdsong in the park, or seen a wonderful view from a train, life then seems extraordinary. I remember a wonderful sunset in North Devon when Rosie and I were on holiday. The colors were tremendous, stunning. I would call that spiritual, partly, because just the experience of the sunset seemed to give life meaning. So I think it may be from these sorts of moments that I've been left with a sense ... mind you nothing more than a glimpse, perhaps, it's even just a feeling that there is another level of life going on ... perhaps, beyond or beneath, or perhaps even alongside the external daily affairs. It's these glimpses or sensations that in a way inspired me to give church another go. As I said earlier, I think I'm not sure if I believe in God, and if I do believe in God what sort of God, but I think there is significance in being alive, perhaps I'm talking about truth ... but I think there is something like that to be found, even when another part of me is sunk in the trivial and a world of apparent unmeaning – if there is such a word.

I'm left feeling that the world I see most of the time cannot be all that there is, or perhaps, it's just about how I look at it ... so that makes me think that there is hidden somewhere a mysterious perhaps otherworldly, and certainly uplifting meaning, which I am suddenly made aware of. It can then feel very poignant, yet it makes me almost believe that the world cannot be just some random thing spinning around in a vast universe, that there is hidden in some still greater depth an unexplained, inspirational meaning, and that's what I'd like to find, and I suppose what I've been searching for over the years. I know life is pretty crazy and some of it plainly ridiculous, but I don't want to believe that it is just all on the surface or absurd. I don't want to believe those scientists talking just about brainwaves ... they always begin what they're saying "it's only" or "it's just" – no – that's not for me! So, I'm up for exploration ... you could say I'm hungry, yes that my heart is hungry, yes, really hungry, to find some meaning before it's too late.

The meaning that comes from facts can only ever be one-dimensional, and the meaning that sets us free gives value to fictional and imaginative processes. The meaning that liberates us is experiential, and so connects with us. We may find great meaning in the liturgy and especially in the Eucharist, but this can only emerge from faith and trust. In other words there needs to be a foundation, good fertile ground, for the experiences to take place. There is a strong history of meaning-making over the centuries, so, for example, medieval mystics remind us of a reflective and contemplative approach to knowledge which enables us simply to connect with what *is*; and in that experience of connection, itself, to find our meaning and become aware of what is sometimes called "presence." Medieval theology put great stress on religious seeking, the Christian search for truth, with Thomas Aquinas standing as a great exemplar for this tradition: "the angelic doctor keeps asking questions as he searches for truth in the universe, in the scriptures, in the teaching of the church ... and part of this Christian search (and, indeed, the principal part) was prayer in which one turned over in one's mind and heart the great mysteries of faith, eventually coming to a profound grasp of their inner meaning."[9]

In the twentieth century, the philosopher and theologian Bernard Lonergan wrote that fundamental theology based on objective statements about the existence of God, the possibility of revelation, the historical existence of Jesus, and other truths that formed the basis of Christian theology, "will no longer do ... In saying this I do not mean that they are no longer true, for they are as true now as they ever were. I mean that they are no longer appropriate."[10] Before any such objective statements, there are, he claimed, subjective experiences, and *this* has to be the basis. This subjective experience is conversion, sometimes taking the form of a meaningful isolated experience, or a continuous or extended process over an entire lifetime – and anything in between. And conversion is meaningful, because it is the experience by which one becomes an authentic human being. The first step for any of us, and perhaps one of life's purposes, is to be authentically human. Conversion to authenticity reaches its highest point where, as Lonergan puts it, one's being becomes a being-in-love, in love with God.

In the next chapter we look at what happens when the hunger for meaning in the heart has become suppressed, and instead there is apathy – a different form of suffering where one is predominantly downhearted and disheartened, yet with a small part still searching.

Chapter 2

Disheartened, and with Hardened Hearts

For the Lord does not see as mortals see; they look on the outward appearance, but the Lord looks on the heart. *1 Samuel 16: 7*

The Lord is near to the broken hearted, and saves the crushed in spirit. *Psalm 34: 18*

Cast away from you all the transgressions that you have committed against me, and get yourselves a new heart and a new spirit! Why will you die, O house of Israel? For I have no pleasure in the death of anyone, says the Lord GOD. Turn, then, and live. *Ezekiel 18: 30–32*

Stuart in the last chapter was hungry and searching, albeit with some mixed feelings, and not very high expectations; in this chapter we look at what happens when our hearts are dulled and depressed. This state of mind is another form of exile, and it comes when one is apathetic and switched off, downhearted and disheartened. With apathy comes a subduing of sensation and a turning away from direct experience, and over time this increasingly becomes a hardening of the heart, so that the possibility of change and positive things happening seems far away. Whilst this appears the opposite of the active searching explored in the previous chapter, the heart is no less hungry, but the spirit of the person is crushed, and this sort of exile carries a desolation and emptiness – a feeling of nothing much, or, as people say: nobody at home, or, whatever. The feeling of deadness and associated isolation and existential loneliness, means that this feels like a place of perpetual winter, a cold wilderness with not much apparent life around, and no obvious fertile ground for new experiences and ideas to grow and develop.

The apathy and hardening will be there for a reason, perhaps to avoid being hurt, and a way of turning away from suffering or pain, but this means that we are not fully present to ourselves and our own needs, and nor are we able to be in real relationship with anybody or indeed anything else. Another reason for hardened hearts might be indifference, not directly because of suffering or neglect, but rather paradoxically because of satiation and complacency. Comfortable in what we have and who we are there is no real need for God. We may see ourselves as religious or spiritual, but this is fueled by surface reasons or habits – the feeling part and the urgency and longing for God have disappeared. In the Bible this condition is understood as having a heart of stone, but the promise is that God will transform this hardened heart into one that is vulnerable and open to what it means to be human – in other words a heart of flesh. This promise is found in two chapters of Ezekiel, Chapter 11 and then later in Chapter 36: 26: "... a new heart I will give you, and a new spirit I will put within you; and I will remove from your body the heart of stone and give you a heart of flesh."

A young woman Carly, and, an older woman Helen, separately describe their situations, and help to explain hearts that are hardened. Firstly, I spoke with Carly who used to be in a young people's group at her church, but now none of it seems relevant or interesting. This is what she says.

Carly

I guess I feel really low about religion, and I don't really know yet what spirituality means. I feel perhaps religion is a bit of a con, pretends to be something and then ... oh I don't know now what I think about it all. I don't go to church although I used to, and most of the time I feel apathetic, perhaps I don't really care anymore. Perhaps I could go again, but at the moment I feel quite low about everything. I'd like to feel less down, but can't seem to get the energy to do anything about it. I think church has a lot of people in it who are doing all right, and feel pleased with who they are and what they've got, but they're not always what they seem.

Just this last Christmas I went into the big church near where I live to have a look around; I don't know why, but I was feeling very fed up with everything, and thought well it's supposed to be a place where you can feel better though I soon realized that I felt so bad about myself that it was only making me feel worse! I don't really know what went wrong, but I was wandering about the place thinking they ought to have a crib, after all it's supposed to be Christmas ... so where's the bloody crib. Then this busybody came bustling up and asked whether I wanted anything. I felt like being really rude, but I just said, "where's the crib?" He then said that they didn't have a crib, and then got hold of my arm, and more or less pushed me round the corner where there was a vicar, standing sorting stuff out, and said that she, the vicar, could explain to me why they didn't have a crib. I just turned away, I could see there was some sort of cribgate row going on and thought I don't want to be used like this, that's not why I came in. So that left me feeling more downhearted, and since then I've just felt nothing much. My life and the world seem to be in such a shit place at present, but I'm now feeling a bit like that old song ... how does it go ... yes "comfortably numb."

Carly then said a little about her spiritual journey up to now:

Carly
Let's see, when I was about fifteen or so, I went to this group that the church set up in the South London suburb where I used to live when I was growing up; I'm dual heritage,

and my dad left when I was young, but luckily there were lots of other kids like me. It was such fun; the leader was this really dynamic alternative young woman ... actually I suppose looking back she was probably in her 30s like I am now, but she dressed like us, and was so casual and really funny. Anyway, her message was that "God is great," and we all chanted this, and then dashed around everywhere telling everyone else that "God is great." I think I went for about two years, and we even went on camping trips and so on. One of the best moments was at the start of it when we came back from helping in a food and furniture bank somewhere up north, and we had these slides of us all lifting sofas and so on, and after showing the slides after the usual church service, we all leapt up on the pews shouting over and over again, "God is great." I remember my mum's face looking a bit surprised, but it was a big buzz. I really believed in God, at least I think I did, but perhaps it was just the fun of everyone – the buzz, the shouting, and nothing to do with God. But when I was about seventeen, I started to get really anxious about going to college, and then what course to do, and what if I couldn't get work, and all that, and somehow just saying, "God is great" didn't shift the tension in my stomach. And I have to say, I then thought it was a bit of a con, like God is great when everything is great, but not great when it's all going wrong. And now, years later, I can remember the buzz, but now it feels more like buzz off. I seem to have had one thing after another going wrong, or not working out, and so I think well there might be a great God, but if so, he's not been great for me.

Let's see what went wrong. Well, first, my darling nan died, she and I had a special bond with each other, and yes she was old, but she suffered really badly, and I hated visiting her seeing her getting more and more ill. Then my dog got some sort of blood poisoning from a tick, and died, and I felt it was my fault because I had taken him into long grass that day and not been careful enough to check on him. I got not very good exam results so didn't get on the course that I wanted, and so went to do a really boring course. I was away from home and felt homesick, and then met this bloke and really fell for him, but that went wrong, and he left me for someone else. Now I'm in a boring job and living on my own. I don't go out much, and I find it hard to trust people, and most of the time I feel really switched off. It's hard to feel interested in anything much, I just feel dull.

I sort of know why I feel so switched off, but don't really want to think about it. I think I've pushed all that stuff far down, but it stays with me all the time. Basically, something happened when I was in the last year of the youth group set-up. There was a lot of talk about what the church thought about sex, they're always banging on about it – excuse the pun ... not really meant – but we had discussions about keeping ourselves pure – whatever that meant – until we were married, and then about same-sex relationships, and what the Bible says and all that. They were really keen on talking about sex anyway, and what you shouldn't do!

I really went along with it (I think mum was relieved!), and could see that some of it made sense, though now I think it's not the business of the church to be telling people what to do or who to do it with ... but, at the time, I felt I was on a mission ... but then this new curate came to the church, and he started to help out at the group, and he was young, well late 20s perhaps early 30s, quite good-looking, so all the girls were a bit silly about him. The youth leader could see what was going on, but just sort of ignored it. Anyway, the curate took part in some of the discussions, saying about how you should wait until you were married, but then when we were away on a trip, he basically cornered me when I was helping him tidy up one evening after the meal, and pushed me into this sort of side room in the place where we were staying, I guess a sort of pantry ... I remember there were tins of tomatoes in there on the shelves, and then he started touching me, and saying that I was leading him on, and how sexy I was ... and all that. I got really confused, and didn't know what to do, you see part of me was flattered that he had found me attractive, but it also seemed against everything that we were being taught, including what *he* was teaching us. I didn't know if he wanted us to be an item like boyfriend and girlfriend or what, so I sort of went along with it, but at the same time I knew it wasn't right. It happened twice on that trip, but afterwards he didn't speak to me really at all.

I worried about it for a while, and decided not to go back to the group or to the church. Anyway I got in such a state that eventually I told my mum, and she complained to the rector of the church, and then she went to the police, but no one was interested because I was over sixteen, and the curate said that it had been consensual. I think he got a rapping for it and was moved to another church, but it was before all the safeguarding stuff came in properly, on the other hand would that have made a difference, as they always defend each other don't they. I felt I was put out to dry and seen as a bad person. I was completely devastated, and it was shortly after that I went away. What really upset me was that the woman group leader didn't take my side; I thought she had been a friend ...

I guess that's why I lost the idea that "God is great," but mostly I tried to push it away, and get on with life. I see now that I was used and betrayed, but I think I was also naïve in thinking that perhaps I interested him – me in myself I mean. But where was the great God when that was happening to me? I think, when I went into the church looking for the crib, I was looking for the innocence again that I used to have in church, but once again I was used, so now I've given up. I don't care.

Carly's heart was broken by disappointment, her absent father, the death of her grandmother and dog, the dull course, and what happened with the curate, and it had all left her fragile. The betrayal and dishonesty disheartened her, but also she hardened herself against further trauma, and became downhearted by life, and then switched off from what it offered. When people have these sorts of experiences the intensity of life and its joys and passions become muted. Being hurt leaves one unwilling to risk further pain, but the danger is that as the walls build up around the heart, we become both insensitive to our own suffering, but also to the suffering of others, even those close to us. This is the comfortably numb state of mind that Carly described so well. When we become cut off in this way, there is no language or any gestures that can be employed to describe feelings, including the feelings when we suffer, or indeed when we are happy. This means that with hardened hearts we lack empathy and sympathy; we might still suffer, but we put up with it, because it doesn't matter anymore – but most of all we try to avoid it.

The child or young person exposed to trauma develops what has been called a false self, which hides and protects the true self by becoming compliant to what is being demanded, and this false self manages the situations; the results are feelings of indifference, and ultimately of futility. The false self appears to be the real person, but it is built on identifications and copies others as a way to further protect the true self.[1] It's about not wearing one's heart on one's sleeve. In other words, it's an avoidance of vulnerability, but also then an avoidance of really feeling alive and real. Carly's apathy was a way of not being hurt further, but it was also an avoidance of living, and this then makes it hard to be open. The indifference is a defense against all the feelings that were stirred up in her in her experiences in the youth group, both when she was compliant to the expectations of the youth group leader, and later, by the confused emotions caused by her sexual encounters with the curate, which she mistook for mutual love.

There is another sort of hardening of hearts, which is linked to the self-satisfaction that Carly complained about in the church; this is also a form of false self. This version is written about in Revelations 3: 15–16. Here, the writer is exhorting Christians: "you are neither hot nor cold. I wish you were either cold or hot. So because you are lukewarm, and neither cold nor hot, I am about to spit you out of my mouth." In this context, the hardening of the hearts that leads to such indifference has also been referred to as banal optimism.[2] In Revelations, the target is those who are successful and prosperous, so much so that they feel that they have no need of God. Their true state of spiritual poverty remains unrecognized. It is a sort of blindness which Helen came to understand. She told me that she and her husband, Roger, have been attending the same church for about thirty years. It's a big city church, but the congregation are quite elderly, and as she describes them perhaps rather set in their ways. Helen says she can see that she is very comfortable going regularly to church, because, as she says, it is what they have always done and so it's what they do. She described to me what happened to her in this way:

Helen

We're quite well off, and I certainly thought I was socially aware, always happy to give a couple of pounds to charity collections, and giving old clothes to charity shops, and I always bake a cake for the church sale, and make soup for the hunger lunches in Lent. It's just I never really gave any of it that much thought. Again, I think it was rather that this is what is expected of you, and so this is what you do. Also, as a church we support a number of mission links, but one

Sunday the whole thing came alive for me in a way that I hadn't experienced before.

One of the team vicars was raising money for an appeal in South Sudan, and he had been talking about the scheme which was a small local one being run by someone he knew, and where he had visited a few months before. I've heard about it before, and I suppose most of what he said went in one ear and came out the other. I was listening, but not really listening if you know what I mean. To tell you the truth, I think we both felt a bit fed up, downhearted about being asked for yet more money. Sometimes I feel that there's too much of that expected, and not enough given back to us ... though I suppose that's not what I should say as a Christian. Usually, I might look in my wallet and bring out a couple of pounds. I've learnt to do that rather than a note – after all, and I know that again this isn't the correct thing to say as a Christian, but if you gave to everyone or every good cause that asks you you'd never have anything left for yourself, and also some of the money gets wasted and all that. Anyway – and this is the truth – I was also thinking, what is the point of giving more money to this conflict-ridden country. It'll just be snapped up by corrupt officials, and they all go on fighting each other – why can't they sort themselves out. But the vicar then asked us to imagine one older man in particular whom he had met when he was out there, and he began to describe him, what he was wearing and how he looked, and a bit about his immediate family and his extended family. And then he said, "if he was standing at the door as you left church today, I know you would be moved by the sight of him, his dignity in the face of adversity and feel compassion. Just imagine it, imagine he's there now."

I don't know what it was, perhaps the words he used, but I suddenly felt terribly ashamed. You see the thing was that I *could* imagine him and I *could* see him in comparison to us with our smart clothes, our going back to lunch then perhaps out for a walk this afternoon, back to our comfortable house, tea, perhaps to watch a film and so on. And I thought how I would feel to be in his place. I found myself thinking, he's probably the same age as me, it could have been me, and what would I feel having no food to feed my family, and having to ask for money in this way. He came alive for me and it all became very real. Needless to say, I gave a lot more than I had been planning, and it seemed to awaken me, and I think Roger, too, was affected. We did talk about it on the way home, and did a bit of research of our own on the situation and tried to get beyond the popular media view and our apathy about knowing what is going on.

As we spoke, Helen had more to say about feeling fed up and downhearted about being asked for money and the general switching off.

Helen
Well, I've thought about it a lot, and do actually think there's only so much you can take. And whatever happened that Sunday, I do still turn off the pictures on the TV if I see ones of starving children, I feel confused about it all, I feel I ought to know about it and as a Christian I ought to give money, but I also feel I want it on my terms, I don't want the advertisers telling me what to feel – though talking about it now perhaps that was what the vicar was doing. No ... I don't think that's quite right ... I think he was sharing what had happened to him when he had gone there, and I didn't feel manipulated by him – I felt moved by what he said. But I think we do have to sometimes block out the pain, not only of what is happening in these places, but perhaps also the pain that is right under our noses. I think I had been going through the motions of giving a little money every now and then to

different causes, but I hadn't felt it, or thought about it. I suppose I felt lukewarm about the whole thing. I felt it was right to give something, but with a sort of resigned feeling which is something like this is what you do, or have to do, when you're people like us.

We do have everything in comparison, but the strange thing was that that Sunday I felt we had nothing. I felt we weren't dignified or noble like that man from Sudan was in the face of suffering. I thought that I, anyway, was ignorant, and careless about all that I've been given. And I felt selfish and rich, well in comparison to people who have nothing. I think in the past I felt a bit frightened about taking all that sort of stuff on ... it's easier to be a bit indifferent, and I suppose you could say that the words of the vicar opened my heart that day, and we both felt something of another person's pain, and strangely our own too. It's not so wonderful having everything when others don't, it doesn't feel that good, and it feels lucky, but also selfish.

Carly and Helen, despite their different stories, are both describing states of false self-organization; ways of keeping aloof or apart from being alive with all that that entails: joy and suffering, pleasure and pain, feeling fully alive. This is a disconnection from authenticity, where one is operating on automatic pilot, and in that sense going through the motions of what it means to be alive. Living in this way is ultimately unsatisfactory, and can lead to depression and feelings of anger and sadness. If we draw back and harden our hearts, then we become emotionally stunted, smaller in our appreciation of ourselves and of one another, and ultimately limited in our relationship with God. It is a retreat from life and from living wholeheartedly. Yet, there still remains deep within us, the special place of God's operation which is our human heart, our inner center and secret inner cave. It may feel hidden even from ourselves, but, as Helen found, and Carly is hoping to find that part of us can always be reached.

Chapter 3

A Heart of Flesh – Being Human

For the human heart and mind are deep. *Psalm 64: 6*

At the edge of your heart the Lord is standing with a tall candle that burns without smoking or melting. The Lord is standing and waiting at your invitation, to bring the candle into your heart and enlighten it, to burn up all the fear in your heart. *St Nikolai Velimirovich in Prayers by the Lake LXXIX*

A new heart I will give you, and a new spirit I will put within you; and I will remove from your body the heart of stone and give you a heart of flesh. *Ezekiel 36:26*

As Helen and her husband, Roger, found, reawakening contact with one's own heart, is, at the same time, about being plunged into the heart of the world, and becoming aware of "the deepest and most neglected voices that proceed from its inner depth."[1] In this chapter, these unwanted and rejected parts of our own hearts are explored first, and then linked to how we feel about ourselves as beings in the world, and our link with the abandoned, ignored and unloved people and parts of creation. Reawakening the heart that has become hardened is about overcoming fear – the fear of who we really are, and how we are in the world. It is about assessing our passion for power and control, and for self-satisfaction – temptations confronted by Jesus in the desert wilderness. It is also about beginning to acknowledge the need to balance the opposites – the good and the bad, the green shoots growing in the stony ground, life in the desert.

Carl Jung said that knowledge of the heart cannot be found in a book, but only through experience, and, invariably, it is in our experiences with others that our own hearts of flesh are revealed. Sometimes this is encouraging, and sometimes more complex and challenging. The final person whose spiritual journey we are following is Frank who was working with the elderly as part of a team involved in day center work and outreach. This is what he has to say about finding out about his heart of flesh ... and, he adds, as a warning: it isn't pretty.

Frank

I've always thought that I was a good person with a kind heart, and in some ways I still believe that, but now I know that there is also another side to me, and that has been a shock. For many years I worked at a desk job, but then the firm was made redundant, so after a few months of trying to find something similar I thought I'd try and go for work that was more meaningful – more socially meaningful. I'd become a Christian in my mid-40s, and believed that it was my duty to help other people, and so that was really the motivation. I took a big cut in income, but at the same time I'd inherited some money when my dad died, and we'd paid off the mortgage, so money wasn't the be all and end all like it used to be. I thought I was a good person, and wanted to do good things.

Anyway to cut a long story short, I ended up at a day center for the elderly, helping initially with everyday activities, and then I was promoted to deputy manager, and that included sorting out the finances and doing some assessments, and so I had a bit more responsibility. I really liked the clients – they were great, especially some of the men who had had interesting lives. I had no problems with any of them, and I found the work stimulating, and at times a bit challenging, but I really felt I'd made a good move.

When I began, the manager was a very experienced old-timer, who ran the place really well so that everyone knew where they were, and what was expected. I was able to pick up quite quickly what my responsibilities were, and I got on well with her. In fact, we more or less ran it together. Unfortunately, she then retired after about a year, and we had a couple of temporary people and I helped out even more ... and, then, in came Katy. I'd actually thought I would get the post as I recognized I was good at the job, I went for the interview and all that ... but, for some reason, I didn't. Katy hadn't been a manager before, although she had worked in a different day center as deputy manager – the same level as me, but she got right under my skin. I suppose I was upset that I wasn't manager ... but she didn't feel real, it was as if she was putting on an act all the time, but she was also really hopeless at managing, leaving me and the volunteers doing everything.

We started off just about okay, but I thought she was patronizing to the clients, and to me. Katy thought she was God's gift to the elderly, and, okay ... it still makes me irritated to think about it all, I can still get worked up about it. So, here's an example, at the day center she would decide that one of the clients needed lots of attention, so, instead of sorting out what the whole group was doing, she would sit with whoever her chosen was for that day, and then the others would feel all left out, and then they'd begin wanting attention, and to know what we were doing that day. I found I was really organizing everything, I might as well have been manager. I think she was stepping outside her role, and almost becoming a social worker.

It was her voice that really annoyed me, I could hear her saying, "oh poooor you and oh how dreeeaadful" ... she has a habit of elongating her vowels, and her voice is all false and so on. I thought that she was just putting it on, and she wasn't efficient either. It also meant that while she was playing this part, I was left dealing with everyone else, and sorting out the volunteers who were making teas and coffees, and it got more and more frantic, because the whole time we were one staff person short, cos she wasn't doing what she was supposed to do.

In the end I lost my rag with her, and said that I thought she should be managing the whole group and helping us sort things out. I said it a couple of times, but then on this dreadful occasion I told her again, she then peered into my face, and said, "oh poooor Frank ... what's the matter ... are you feeling it's all tooooo much." I couldn't help myself, I grabbed her arm, and pulled it, and said to stop it. I had to walk away from her in the end, as I thought I might really hurt her. I was just so angry. I could feel this rush of rage – I know now what they mean when people talk about seeing red. When I came back in, it was clear she had been crying, and all the volunteers were looking awkwardly at me. We then had to have a talk, and I tried to explain how I felt, but she was still making me feel like a bully and a thug, and I had behaved badly. I was quite shaken too, and frightened by myself, if the truth be told. I haven't felt as angry as that since I was a kid.

The thing is that in the past I've always tried not to rock the boat, and I'm not used to confrontation ... but I like things to be controlled ... Also, I like to be seen as Mr Nice Guy, and after my explosion with Katy I couldn't pretend I was that anymore. I knew that I could be as angry as anyone, and driven to violence – well, I was violent when I pulled her arm, and that was a real shock. I thought – and you're a Christian too!

As Frank discovered, the human heart is deeper than any of us can really understand, and all sorts of different, often contradictory feelings can co-exist. Self-deception and denial can prevent this realization, so it can feel shocking how when we are feeling elated, a sudden sense of depression can emerge; or when we are feeling loving, a destructive viciousness can fleetingly come into view. Although religion emphasises the command to love, human love is ambiguous, as all relationships include a variety of emotions; the opposite is always present, and to ignore this leads to much confusion and unhappiness. If Frank had been able to accept that he had mixed feelings and was not having to be "nice" all the time, perhaps he would have been better able to turn his anger into something a bit more constructive, rather than lashing out.

All of us find it easier to divide things into good and bad, black or white, and so on, preferring to ignore or deny that in reality things are more nuanced, and that both black and white, both good and bad are possible, and even that there are shades of gray and times when we are just being neutral. Frank could not believe that in doing what he felt was meaningful work, he said it was his "duty" to help others, he could feel so negative, especially when his self-image was one of being friendly and nice and kind to the elderly. The opposite emotions are bound to come out in one way or another if they are actively suppressed. Acceptance of the mixture of emotions within each of us is the first step towards understanding what really goes on in a heart of flesh, in the human heart, and that recognition can be frightening.

Carl Jung understood that we would rather not know about the negative within us, and he called this the shadow; the parts of ourselves that we push into the background, into the shadow, and pretend do not exist. Ignoring the parts of ourselves that we disown, means that we have a tendency to push or project these onto others, sometimes in the form of prejudice and certainly distancing ourselves from them. Jung wisely understood that without acknowledging all the parts of our hearts we remained blind. He wrote in a letter: "But your vision will become clear only when you look into your heart. Without, everything seems discordant; only within does it coalesce into unity. Who looks outside dreams, who looks inside awakes."[2]

Children know the depths of the heart and the co-existence of love and hate, but they are taught to cover up their feelings, and censor their words, and the immediacy of the experience is lost in the sophistication of our focus on civilized manners. The Jesuit priest Carlos G. Valles tells the story of visiting the parents of a young boy, and asking the young boy who had been playing with his toys on the floor: What are you going to be when you grow up?[3] The conversation had been about the boy's future studies, and Valles was trying to include the boy in the discussion. Immediately, the boy replied that he wanted to be a doctor. The answer reflected what the parents wanted for their small son, who had obediently replied mirroring their enthusiasm. Valles, as he reflected later, had foolishly prolonged the interview:

> I asked the boy with a show of interest that charged the trivial question with feigned importance, "And what are you going to do when you are a doctor?" The answer came swift and definite, in clear words and cutting intonation: "When I am a doctor I'll give Daddy and Mummy an injection and I'll kill them!" Daddy and Mummy laughed. I laughed. The boy did not laugh and continued to play with his toys. The interview was over.

Clearly the laughter covered the embarrassment of the ruthless message, but the boy's daydream was about how to kill his parents; as Valles describes it, "the needle of hatred in the heart of love. The shadow of death in the home of life. Murder in the mind of a child. And unbelieving bewilderment in his well-meaning parents."

Getting in touch with the ever present rage and anger in childhood is a necessity, if we are to grow into balanced adults. Getting rid of the anger means that the child can move on, but the danger is that the feelings are suppressed, and seen as a passing tantrum rather than the reminder that there are complicated emotions within every one of us, religious or not, and such feelings have to be taken into account if we want to understand ourselves and others.

For Frank, it was intolerable to think that he, Mr Nice Guy, had hate inside him. Never! Yet there it was rushing up and feeling uncontrollable, buried under social convention, duty, Christian love and respectability, and good manners, but very much alive in the depths of the heart. One of the difficulties to emerge from simplistic religious teaching is that God is the pure and good God portrayed in contrast to the sullied and sinful people who stand abject and sorry waiting for redemption and forgiveness. People who do this then become good as distinct from the others who do not turn to God who are bad. When Matthew records Jesus saying: "Be perfect, therefore, as your heavenly Father is perfect" (Matthew 5: 48) a better translation is to be whole or mature in the sense that we recognize and integrate all aspects of ourselves.

In our hearts there are a whole mass of feelings, often contradictory, and sometimes conflictual that we can experience at any moment, and sometimes, like in Frank's outburst, they are unbidden and unexpected. Immediate frustrations alongside hurtful memories and resentments, past pain and present indignation, and also sudden joy and pleasures all contribute to mixed feelings. Christians are especially prone to banish the word hate from their vocabulary – after all didn't Jesus tell us to love one another, and to love our enemies. So, as Christians, we are told that we do not hate people no matter how annoying or unpleasant they are, nor how hurtful or abusive. We can perhaps say that we dislike, or avoid or reject that person, but sometimes those statements can only be said in a quiet whisper. It is anathema to acknowledge or recognize hatred towards another as it is seen as unchristian, unethical and inappropriate to hate anyone. However, we can voice hatred easily about things that annoy us, "I hate loud music in shops," "I hate that television program," and so on. The statements carry a feeling that is well over the top, because somehow the feeling has to emerge even through lighter topics. The fear is that under pressure the emotion pops out.

After Helen's realization that she was rather uninvolved, she told me that she decided to enter more fully into the life of the church, and so she enrolled to help with the children's groups at church. She explained why she wanted to do this.

Helen

Well I'm doing it, I think, for a number of reasons. I did, yes, I did feel that the incident I described to you before about giving money was a bit of a wakeup call, and I suppose I thought that I ought to contribute more to the church. I couldn't quite think what, there's always coffee and tea rotas and flowers, and so on, but, actually there's a group that always does that, and to tell you the truth it seemed a bit boring, but then I thought that I don't like the way that children don't know their Bible anymore, so I thought well I could go on the rota for the children's groups. It's a funny business as the church is always speaking about how they value their children, but there's very few of us on that rota, people say that they want to be in the church not out in a side room, or they've done their bit with children ... and well there's not that many children now either, but I decided I could do that ... as Roger says, I have the best of intentions, though he says he doesn't understand why I'm doing it!

So, I now lead the small group of 3–5-year-olds, probably every six weeks, and usually I enjoy it because I am determined to help the church teach children about the Bible. It's not always the same children, but there's a core group of two or three little girls who come. The incident that worried me happened a few weeks ago, when this girl came who was just visiting on holiday. For a start, she had a strange name, not the usual sort of name – a fancy one and was wearing, I suppose, some dressing up clothes – like a princess, she told me ... but that upset me because I thought the parents should have dressed her better for coming to church.

But when I started the story – it was about the poor woman who gave her last coin into the temple coffer, and in contrast the rich man who gave lots but out of his huge wealth, well this girl she kept asking questions. I thought at first it was good, as it showed she was interested and listening, but then she kept interrupting me, and she was wriggling around on her chair too which began to be annoying. I didn't do anything, but I kept thinking I don't like this child ... and I don't think she likes me. I had made a container with a gold cloth and some toy money to show the place where the money was put in the temple, and she kept peering in and taking the money out, and then the others copied her, and started doing it too, but I wanted them to get on with their coloring – which admittedly they did, but the whole thing stirred something up for me, and I have to say put me in a bad mood for the rest of the day. I knew I was upset by it, but I couldn't quite understand it at first. But it did make me think. I also found I couldn't sleep as the feeling of really disliking her seemed to stay with me for ages, and it seemed especially wrong not to like a child, definitely unchristian.

Helen did think about it as she was shocked by the depths of her feelings, and she knew it had to be something to sort out as she didn't want to feel so taken over by her dislike. It seemed such a contrast to how she usually was – certainly not like the switched off Helen from before. She came up with this reflection, helped by a discussion with her daughter who was training as a counselor.

I laughed about it when I sorted it out, as I felt the story from the Bible that I was teaching held the key to understanding what had happened. I thought, when I'm teaching although I think I want to do it, I do often have other thoughts as it can sometimes feel as if you've been forgotten out at the back of the church, while everyone else is in the main body of the building. In fact, that day, I wasn't supposed to be leading the group, it wasn't my turn on the rota, but a few days before someone had rung me to ask if I could step in as the person doing it was poorly. So, of course, I said yes, though I had only just done it a week or so before. I think I then felt like the poor widow giving everything that I have. Well, actually, as my daughter pointed out to me, I was feeling resentful, about being taken for granted because it was assumed that I would step in, and, quite honestly, I wouldn't have known how to say "no" – and as an aside my daughter says that she sees that as a problem for me. Well I know in the story, the woman gets praised, and Jesus sees her sacrifice, but when that girl joined the group with her fancy name and princess costume it seemed like in a strange way she was like the man who had so much. She wasn't sitting quietly, she was really lively and bright and smart, and I wanted to punish her for that. I really wanted to punish her for being so unconcerned about how she looked, and how she behaved.

When I talked it over with my daughter, and she is really great like that – thank goodness for the counseling course – I could see that although I was doing the right thing by agreeing to lead the class, perhaps it was too soon after I had just done it, but I now think that some of what I was feeling that day went back to my own childhood, where I had to sit absolutely still reading the Bible on a Sunday, as my parents were part of a very strict sect, and I was never allowed to wear anything but sensible and rather dull clothes. I thought I had left all that behind, but something about that girl brought it all up again. She was like I couldn't ever be, and I thought that she should be controlled more, perhaps that she should have been made to be like I was at her age! Oh dear, I can see it now, and I felt relieved when I talked it through, because what I didn't like was how horrid I felt towards her, and she sort of knew it too, which I do feel sorry about because perhaps it will mean that she won't want to go to church again, or read a Bible – just the very opposite of what I was wanting to happen. The whole event was really food for thought, and made me think how much goes on inside our heads!

Helen's account of her struggle with mixed feelings raises the question: What might it mean to love our enemies? Revd James Martin[4] introduces the idea of loving our enemies with a joke:

A priest is giving a homily based on Jesus's command to love your enemies.

"Now," he says, "I'll bet that many of us feel as if we have enemies in our lives," he says to the congregation. "So, raise your hands," he says, "if you have many enemies." And quite a few people raise their hands. "Now raise your hands if you have only a few enemies." And about half as many people raise their hands. "Now raise your hands if you have only one or two enemies." And even fewer people raised their hands. "See," says the priest, "most of us feel like we have enemies."

"Now raise your hands if you have no enemies at all." And the priest looks around, and looks around, and finally, way in the back; a very, very old man raises his hand. He stands up and says, "I have no enemies whatsoever!" Delighted, the priest invites the man to the front of the church. "What a blessing!" the priest says. "How old are you?"

"I'm 98 years old, and I have no enemies." The priest says, "What a wonderful Christian life you lead! And tell us all how it is that you have no enemies."

"All the bastards have died!"

Helen's curiosity had been suppressed as a child, but as her heart began to open out from a state of indifference, she felt more in touch with what she really felt, and, importantly, her curiosity resurfaced. Uncovering this, as Helen did, and discovering more about why we feel the way we do is about having a heart of flesh. The heart of flesh contains energy and passion with a whole range of feelings. Some will be extremely painful and the others joyful, so the inner psychological and spiritual work is about the need to take responsibility for how the past and present are owned and registered in the mind. Having a heart of stone might seem easier, but to be alive and open to God, we need the heart of flesh with all the different feelings and ambiguities that that involves.

Chapter 4

A Contrite Heart

Yet even now, says the Lord, return to me with all your heart, with fasting, with weeping, and with mourning; rend your hearts and not your clothing. *Joel 2: 12–13*

A broken and contrite heart Oh God, you will not despise. *Psalm 51: 17*

The phrase a contrite heart and the idea of repentance appear in different parts of the Bible, for contrition seems to elicit God's favor in the sense that the hardened and disheartened person begins to awaken, and to open their heart enough to become attentive to a sense of brokenness, and associated vulnerability. The Hebrew and Greek word contrite can also include the meanings of crushed, crippled, or broken. While the phrase, a contrite heart, may be familiar from religious texts it's not an expression we usually use now in the twenty-first century. So how can it be understood: Harry Williams saw repentance as an inevitable part of all human life, whether people think of themselves as religious or not, "its root is the discovery by us that we are keeping a large part of ourselves locked away and hence that we are living much more superficially than we need."[1] In Richard Coles' autobiography he recounts the disapproval he expressed to his spiritual director about the behavior of fellow ordinands, whilst he was training at Mirfield College of the Resurrection.

Advent is traditionally a time for repentance so we went off to see our spiritual directors, monks of the community, one by one ... I told him about what had been going on, which I was sure he knew about, and let rip about the foolishness and unkindness of some of the people who I had to live with and work it out with. "Go on," he said. I paused and thought and said, "I'm not as kind as I thought I was. I'm not as brave as I thought I was. I'm not as tolerant as I thought I was. I'm not as clever as I thought I was. I'm not as honest as I thought I was." There was a pause and he said, "Oh, that's good."

And it was. The problem was not the awfulness of others, the problem was the awfulness of me, so stuck in my self-regard that I had not seen how marginal my angst was to what was happening all around me. And the only thing I could do about it was deal with my own awfulness, because the awfulness of others was for them to deal with and, besides, how could I even begin to see straight until I had cleared my own eyes of obstruction.[2]

To make repentance and contrition meaningful in any way, one would need a capacity for self-reflection, and enough motivation and ability to begin to explore one's inner world, and then think about how we interact with one another in the external world. In other words, it is about acknowledging different states of mind, and then beginning to take responsibility to understand what has happened both to us, and, also, within us, and how this affects the way we feel, and think, and behave. To have a contrite heart means to own the way we are, and to wish to change or in some way remedy and heal this; it is a process of discovery. It is about accepting our vulnerability and brokenness, and in this frame of mind is a blessing, as it suggests the beginning of a real relationship with God; one where we know our need for God and for his mercy, and so can be open enough to receive it. Before this, we may have to go through stages of shame and guilt, self-doubt and confusion. One of the effects of getting to know ourselves and beginning to appreciate the shadow emotions that have previously been pushed far away, is that we are then dealing with feelings – in other words emotions that have been experienced, acknowledged and so partially processed. Such confrontation requires coming to terms with responses such as shame and guilt, which when explored further can be seen as acting to cover deeper feelings of brokenness and distress. Awareness of these inner depths can lead us to a place of humility, which takes us back to our foundations, back to basics, to "our earth" and perhaps then to recognition of the ground of our being – to God.

Before his conversion to Roman Catholicism, and, whilst still a student, Thomas Merton writes about the shame he felt after nights out drinking and listening to jazz when he was waiting for a dawn bus to take him back home:

[W]eary and ready to fall, lighting the fortieth or fiftieth cigarette of the day ... The thing that depressed me most was the shame and despair that invaded my whole nature when the sun came up, and all the labourers were going to work ... with some rational purpose before them. This humiliation and sense of my own misery and of the fruitlessness of what I had done was the nearest I could get to contrition. It was the reaction of nature. It proved nothing except that I was still, at least morally alive: or rather that I had still some faint capacity for moral life in me. The term "morally alive" might obscure the fact that I was spiritually dead.[3]

The word shame comes from a word that means to cover, that is, to hide. And shame truly is the hidden feeling. The parts of ourselves we wish to hide are the shameful parts, and we also wish to hide the fact that we are ashamed. If we can't prevent it, we hide it. In common language when we talk about embarrassment, humiliation, or mortification we are talking about shame. Once again, we are talking of the hidden objectionable parts of ourselves that we prefer to hide rather than to know. When I next met with Carly, shame was one of the feelings that she wanted to share when we talked further about what had happened with the curate in the youth group.

Carly

People didn't say it out loud although the group leader rather implied it, but I know back then that they thought that the whole business with the curate was my fault, and that I ought to be ashamed of myself. Even I thought later, well – shame on you! Meaning shame on me! I just felt so exposed through the whole business, and I'm not sure that deep down that has ever really gone away. In some ways he broke my heart, because I really liked him. I know it has made me hate myself, though I am now trying to be kinder – yes to myself. The other thing I'm ashamed about is that it's hard to be joyful or happy, even if it's a nice day or something good has happened, and I think that is anti-life if you know what I mean. So I'm ashamed of being ashamed. I think though that that makes me lonely, as if there's another me that is trying to get out, and needs to just connect with someone again.

There is an excellent example of shame as a soul-eating emotion (Carl Jung called it that because shame tends to worm its way right to our very core and remain long after any event that caused it), and that comes from the story of Adam and Eve in the garden of Eden. This biblical story of the expulsion from paradise is the most influential myth in our culture dealing with shame. In it, we are told that, after eating from the tree of knowledge, Adam and Eve suddenly felt ashamed of their nakedness. Before this incident, they had been naked without feeling ashamed. But the fruit of knowledge gave them the capacity to distinguish between "I and Thou" subject and object, and thus they awoke to the realization that they were two separate beings – her naked body was different from his, as was plain to see. Feeling ashamed, and ashamed in front of God about what they had done, they stitched together garments of fig-leaves to cover their private parts. When Adam told God that he was afraid, and hid because he was naked, God asked him: Who told you that you were naked? Or in other words: Who told you that you were bad? John Jacob Raub sees this rhetorical question as the most fundamental question ever put to humankind, he points out that it is not God who makes the judgments against Adam and Eve, but rather Adam who has judged himself, and that this judgment against himself was the result of eating from the tree of good *and* bad.[4] In their actions, humankind has chosen to be like the gods, and so by necessity we judge ourselves as being not what we should be or ought to be – as *not* being like the gods. Here is the setting up of the false standard of either good or bad, with the options of either seeing ourselves as naked, as bad, as guilty and wrong, and so we are ashamed; or there is an alternative which is to project all that negative stuff onto others instead which can offer temporary relief. As will be explored later, a better solution is to appreciate that we, like everyone else, are good *and* bad, happy *and* sad, which is a cause for understanding and integration rather than blame and shame.

Shame arises with the awareness of being exposed, and seen by others, and so it motivates us to protect our intimacy, physical and emotional, under the cover of a symbolic fig-leaf or loincloth, to keep for ourselves what is no one else's business. In this way, it reinforces interpersonal distinctness and a sense of one's own individual identity, yet underneath this the fear is about vulnerability, and exposure of where we are defenseless. In this way, it confirms that we are apparently different from each other with our own identity, but at the same time, shame actually acts as a powerful inducement toward conformity. We all work quite hard to avoid shame and that can lead to deception. Shame and deceit are interwoven into a vicious circle; shame leads to deceit, deceit produces an underlying sense of helplessness, which then produces more deceit and self-condemnation, which produces even more shame, but underneath there is a fragile and vulnerable part – the true self. Thus the antidote to the experience of shame is the quest (or struggle) for acceptance – of the flawed self, by self or by the other. For Carly, left with powerful and debilitating feelings of shame, the power comes from the difficulty of speaking about what had happened, and also the way that the events were handled, and the lack of responsibility taken by the curate, and indeed the church generally. This meant that Carly took the moral responsibility, and so was left confused and disgusted by herself. Here Carly's shame was to do with her own sense of exposure, her sexuality, and the feeling that she had failed expectations in some way, so it was associated with feelings of weakness; her guilt was about what actually took place. It has been said that to confront shame – something we would prefer to flee from – requires a leap of faith, and part of that leap involves acknowledging a need for healing, and a belief that despite everything there is a part of oneself worth saving. This is then, a good point to pick up Carly's story as she tried again to see if the church near her could offer anything. After the Christmas visit, she was not that hopeful, but she had another go before Easter when she decided to go to an evening Maundy Thursday service. This is her description of what happened.

Carly

I was feeling pretty low again, and I felt in a strange way compelled to go into the church, though I wasn't expecting much ... what I liked was that there weren't that many people, no one was fussing and people seemed caught up in themselves, and, serious. I remembered what Maundy Thursday was about, and I found the service really meaningful, and I suppose the betrayal by Judas, and then the disappointment about the weakness of the disciples really connected with me. No one was being jolly, or forcing others to be jolly, in fact it felt quite sad which tuned in with my mood that evening. There was a foot washing ceremony, and everyone was invited up, but quite a few people looked uncomfortable and didn't move out of the pews. So I decided not to go at first, but then at the last minute I thought, why not, I've nothing to lose, and at the very least I'll have clean feet! They'd arranged it so that you had your feet washed, and then you in turn washed someone else's feet. It was just who you were next to in the queue, and thankfully I was next to this older woman. Strangely, I found myself feeling a bit tearful as she washed and dried my feet so carefully, it was like being a little girl again. At first, I was embarrassed that she might find my feet disgusting, but she was completely focused on doing it in this gentle and observant way. I felt humbled by it, but also accepted for who I am. It had a weird – in a good way – effect on me, and so I then tried to do the same when it was my turn to wash her feet. It was very exposing, but it felt quite safe, and it was all done in silence – no words, no social stuff and no expectations. And I went back on Good Friday –it was a breakthrough.

What was happening here as Carly took off her shoes? At the conscious level she was taking part in this ancient ritual instituted by Jesus, but the symbolism goes further. Taking off shoes is reminiscent of walking on holy ground, so it is in part also a sign of respect, but it can also stand as a metaphor for laying down the superficial everyday part of ourselves. The persona is the part that is presented to the world, which can act as a mask or a disguise for the real person underneath – the true self. Being barefoot is about laying down the burden of who we are, and in itself conveys a sense of freedom. This stripping away is also about removing things – perhaps privilege or status, though in Carly's case it was about removing the hard shell surrounding her heart. Being barefoot is a sign of purity and vulnerability.

Remember what it is like to take off shoes and socks and walk towards the sea, the feeling of the sand becoming increasingly wet, and the first delicious feel of the cold seawater lapping around. Carly, even in her state of depression and distress, was able to, barefoot, step outside her normal concerns, and be in the moment, particularly noticing the gentle way in which her feet were dried. In the biblical account, Jesus uses the feet washing to show love; it is a form of service but also through the actions God shows us that we are each his beloved child – unconditionally loved, no matter how ashamed or guilty we may feel.

Religion has not always understood about the experiences that make us feel ashamed; in fact often the church has increased shame in a way that means the person cannot be open, and so confront the source of the pain and discomfort. This is partly to do with the emphasis on sin and that if we are encouraged to project the powerful, productive, good and reasonable aspects of the self into the all-powerful and all-good God, then one is left only with the opposites of these virtues. Carl Jung, thought that this perhaps explains why so many atrocities and absurdities are committed by the devoutly religious, so he argued for the importance of appreciating that God – if transcending all the opposites contained in the world must by definition include such opposites. Jung was adamant that we recognize the negative both in God and in the Self, for God's completeness, and, the fact that the divine is the template for the human personality necessitates the existence of the divine shadow and so coming to terms with our personal and collective shadow. Whatever the dynamic, the church has certainly unhelpfully played on guilt, and Harry Williams criticizes the way, "It impresses guilt upon people ever more savagely so that it may then graciously offer them the free gift of salvation." It then becomes a form of moral blackmail.[5] For most of us can manufacture enough shame and guilt about ourselves without an extra helping from the church, where there is a lot of talk about sin.

If we are asked to repent of our sins what does this mean? How can sin be understood? The writer, Franz Kafka, called impatience our only sin; it's something we're born with so his version of original sin as impatience casts its shadow over all that we do and all that we enjoy. "It's the worm at the core of the shiniest apple. We want happiness and we want it now, yesterday even"[6] – it means we're looking ahead, and never in the present moment. Generally Jung, saw the use of the words sin and evil as merely emphatic expressions of an emotional negative reaction, and terms that can be used randomly. As he writes, no one can define what evil is in itself as: "There is nothing which at times cannot be called evil," rather he sees it as "the black fiend ever working in man's nature" and, importantly, universally present in each one of us, whereas sin is usually seen as a deviation from a particular moral code or external law. Jung thought that this superficial meaning of sin was of less interest than the sin of our lack of awareness and unconsciousness, this was the sin of which we needed to repent.[7]

His view is similar to that of Thomas Merton, who saw the real sin as a betrayal of inner freedom, a failure to respond to inner truth. This he sees as a violation of the inmost laws of his being, which are also then a violation of the laws of God, who dwells within him. This means that sin is the experience of "having been deeply and deliberately false to my own inmost reality, my likeness to God."[8] With this definition sin becomes something deeply meaningful as an offence against what is true and real, a failure to be present, and aware of the reality that is in us, and in the world. It is a failure to know our potential, and an obscuring of the spiritual journey towards God and towards the true self. This sort of sin would not feature in a criminal court, but rather is destructive of our relationship with one another, with ourselves and ultimately with God. Carlos Valles describes it as going around in the world with thick veils before our faces that hide our true preferences, our real feelings, our opinions or our reactions.

We disguise and dissemble and hide and cover our true image with the hundred masks of formalism and simulation. We do not meet face-to-face but mask-to-mask, and can go through life hardly meeting anybody in truth. We miss the beauty and wealth and wisdom and joy and warmth and love of real persons in real life. And we move away, disappointed and frustrated in our expectations and our hopes.[9]

The task is to dare to reveal ourselves – shadow and all – rather than suppress and deny. After all, if one knows oneself even a little, one knows feelings of anger and frustration, and then it is possible to harness the energy involved into something constructive, rather than mindlessly take destructive action. It has been argued that the opposite of sin is not virtue, but faith – not a faith based on doctrine, but faith in life and the life force – which in Christian language is a faith in God. If I try hard to be good, then the part I am trying to organize and discipline can only be the part that I am aware of. Ironically, it's in the seeing of me as only this one small part which according to both Jung and Merton, is then the root cause of sin. Exhortations to repent, and amend, mean that it is all concentrated on this little bit of me that I know as against the other parts of me that I don't know. If I have faith, then I will also believe that I am more than I know, as indeed God is more than I can know. My dependence is then on something I do not know and cannot control – God. This, strangely, is a form of freedom, as I am then less on guard against myself, and the increasing awareness of what I am will grow and the more it grows the less I am bound to sin.

Perhaps this is what Jesus meant when he teaches about the danger of riches, especially to the disciples who were materially poor. Harry Williams understood such riches to mean the self-image and self-importance that we each build up, and organize, and manipulate, and that then dominates and oppresses all the other parts of one's self.

> In spite of our Lord's warning that it is easier for a camel to go through the eye of a needle that for a rich man to enter the kingdom of God, we all of us spend a great deal of our time accumulating riches like crazy.[10]
>
> Self-awareness of all the different parts of our inner world, leads to the discarding of the illusion that the self who lords it over all the other parts of one's self is important in any finally important sense. For the structure built on these sorts of false riches is "always in a precarious state. Underneath the confidence is the fear of it tumbling down like a house of cards."

It seems that Jesus recognized how we can imprison ourselves through self-image, and yet, we are reminded that we are not alone in this human condition:

> Slowly slowly
> Comes Christ through the ruins
> Seeking the lost disciple.[11]

Christ shares our human grief, opening doors when, like Carly, it is least expected, and urging us to turn to an attitude of trustful receptivity to life, and to "a me" that is mysterious and unknown. A contrite heart is the start of a movement of a conscious turning back towards God from whom we are obscured, and from whom we feel that we are separated. We are invited into relationship with God, who is creating who we are by means of which we are largely unaware. Therefore, God's forgiveness really means an acceptance of all parts of me – including the shadow, ugly and distorted though it may be. Perhaps, forgiveness can be described as God's acceptance also of our potentiality, seeing below the surface persona to another part, which includes all the potential to become more like him – surely, then, this is the idea of Christ becoming formed in us. The contrite heart is merely the beginning.

Chapter 5

Broken-Hearted

David was stricken to the heart ... *1 Samuel 24: 5*

God is witness of their inmost feelings, and a true observer of their hearts. *Wisdom of Solomon 1: 6b*

Wait for the Lord; be strong, and let your heart take courage; wait for the Lord! *Psalm 27: 14*

Everyone has a sacred story, and the passion narrative of Jesus' betrayal, abandonment and crucifixion is not just an account referring to past events, it is also our story, and it is only if we can accept this that the account will reveal anything to us. For the cross is forever present and forever contemporary; it metaphorically happens to everyone sooner or later. When Jesus cries that he feels forsaken by God, it is the pain of the person who feels totally isolated, when life leaves one feeling unlovable and locked up in private misery; however, it is also true that Good Friday means that when we feel this, we are able to understand that we are no longer alone, but sharing an experience that God himself has.

> What, therefore the cross of Christ demonstrates to us, is that, in spite of all evidence to the contrary both outside us and within us, reality is not hostile to us but absolutely on our side, ready to stand by us and take our part at whatever cost.[1]

However, sometimes it is hard to believe that we can get through whatever has happened to shake our sense of who we are; this was Frank's experience. Earlier Frank shared his dismay and despair at the event that had taken place at his work, and he now describes what happened next.

Frank

Unfortunately, or fortunately, I was suspended from my work after the incident at the day center while an enquiry took place. I can see now that it was quite right. Actually, I had a dreadful fright because I thought at one point, Katy was going to pursue criminal charges against me – for ABH, actual bodily harm, though she didn't, and nor did the organization. The enquiry took a couple of months, and during that time I really suffered. I'm sure that sounds terrible as I wasn't the wronged party, but I just felt so guilty, and, yes, so deeply ashamed. I also felt anxious about the future, and how I would earn money and all that. I didn't know what to do, and I was too ashamed to mention it to my vicar, Elaine ... I thought she might take against me as Katy was female, and it really was inexcusable what I did. Even at home, I felt there were difficulties ... and perhaps I have at times in the past been overbearing with my wife, and perhaps with my son – though I need to quickly say that I have never ever been physically aggressive towards them, and would not be ... but perhaps a bit controlling, I can see it now ... and perhaps a bit center stage.

Stopping work, I felt abandoned, didn't really know what to do to pass the time, and that didn't help the anxiety, I even had a couple of panic attacks which I wouldn't wish on anyone, it seemed to be about just getting through the day. It's ironic really, when you work full time you long for the weekends and holidays, but when something like this happens, I just wanted to be back at work, doing anything, quite honestly. Anyway, at the end of the formal enquiry, and I did get a lot of support from the union, and had a legal representative, so actually all that took up quite a bit of time, but after the enquiry ended, I agreed to go for some counseling and anger management. Also, it was decided that I couldn't go back to work at the center, nor did I want to, they might have found me somewhere else, but I had lost heart with the whole thing. So I resigned, and eventually I got a job doing admin for an organization that runs a few charity shops in the area, and I've stuck at that now for a while. It's okay, and it gives me space to think about how I respond to things, especially when I am feeling under pressure and frustrated. You see, I went to a therapist in the end who specializes in anger and aggression, and I've been seeing him now for a while. I wanted to understand why I had reacted in the way I did, and not just deal with the surface stuff. I wanted to get to the heart of it.

For quite a while, I felt, as I've said, guilty and began to hate myself; I thought I needed to punish myself, and part of it was that I felt separated from God. I felt what I had done was unforgiveable, and particularly burdensome because I had thought I was doing my work, and indeed my duty as a Christian. One of the first things that helped me with this in the therapy was trying to understand where this burden of duty and "oughts and shoulds" came from. The therapist was saying stuff like I was trying to live up to unreal expectations and desires, so something had to give. I was suppressing all the mixed feelings that were inside me, and then it sort of exploded, and that afterwards the guilt, self-hate and punishment were inevitable. Another insight was that I was easily threatened; I was threatened by Katy because she made me feel I was lacking something, well she did get the job over me! Perhaps there was also some sexism in there, I didn't like my boss being a woman – I've thought about that quite a bit too. Anyway, I still maintain she was annoying, but, okay I let her get to me. I think I began to feel like a failure inside, and then I hated myself, and for that moment rage seemed the only option. Of course, I now bitterly regret it, and my lack of insight. It has all been heart-rending. It's affected me, and of course the family too. I think we are only now beginning to get over it.

And just to add to the mix I have at times got in touch with my anger towards God ... I know that sounds a bit rich, but I did think I was doing *his* work, and this is the thanks I get for it. Why didn't God stop this happening? It's taken me a while to see that breaking down in this way, and everything that's happened *may*, and I emphasize *just may* at some point turn out to be a breakthrough, well that's what the therapist says!

Frank's overt anger was an exaggerated version of the little flashes of anger born out of frustration or hostility that we all experience during an average day. If this is suppressed and pushed away, because as Christians we feel we shouldn't be angry rather than acknowledging it, the emotion becomes all the more powerful. Learning to live with our shadowy demons, in other words accepting the mixed feelings that are part of being human, diffuses their power, and enables the energy behind the feelings to be used in a more constructive way. St Paul was well aware of this. It's not clear what his trouble was – perhaps it was anger too – but he lamented: "For I do not do what I want, but I do the very thing I hate ... But in fact it is no longer I that do it, but sin that dwells within me" (Romans 7: 15, 17). Here Paul is struggling, aware of what is going on, and knowing his need for help: "Wretched man that I am! Who will rescue me from this body of death? Thanks be to God through Jesus Christ our Lord" (Romans 7: 25). After all, the Gospel does not tell us to annihilate our anger, and Jesus did not annihilate his, nor does it tell us to repress it and hide it away in our unconscious. William Johnston the Jesuit monk and writer writes:

Rather must we transform it (or, more correctly, let God

62

transform it) into a seeking of the kingdom of God and His justice. And when this is done, destructive anger becomes just anger. It becomes the anger of a Mahatma Gandhi, a Martin Luther King, a Dorothy Day, a Thomas Merton, a Lech Walesa ... Overpowering and uncontrollable anger has becomes an enlightened passion for justice. But this has happened ... through a profound conversion of heart which is nothing less than mystical.[2]

These difficult emotions become transformed into their opposites, and so the demons become our friends, or at the very least, well-known and accepted acquaintances. Having an awareness of the powerful emotion of anger without accepting it can often lead to another demon, which is anxiety, and sometimes extreme anxiety manifested in panic attacks. Frank was left feeling anxious – his self-esteem, and his sense of who he was, had been greatly shaken, and there was the added uncertainty about his job prospects, and the fallout affecting his home life. In some ways, Frank's anxious insecurity had led to his feelings of competitiveness, and his need to prove himself with the manager of the day center, and had fueled his angry outburst. And, of course, anxiety affects our relationship with God too. It can drive us to all sorts of manipulations, and can drive out faith where we cannot believe that we are loved and protected by God no matter what we feel. In such a frame of mind we are, as Johnston terms it, practical atheists, which is why the Gospel, consistently links anxiety to lack of faith and urges us to relinquish fear: "Do not let your hearts be troubled, and do not let them be afraid" (John 14: 27). For many, it is easier to accept a physical illness than mental instability, but emotional breakdown can be a vulnerable opening-up that can lead to insights and breakthrough. As in Frank's situation, it can be one way in which a constructed sense of ourselves begins to fall apart, and then be seen as a rather superficial or false self hiding or protecting what we might call the naked realities of the heart. Thomas Merton had experiences of anxiety and depression while he was still out in the world, and even within the monastery experienced the pressure of overwork and stress; this experience contributed to Merton's growing realization that solitude is necessary: "To belong to God I have to belong to myself. I have to be alone – at least interiorly alone." Rediscovering solitude, Merton turns to Psalm 54: 5–9 (Anglican Psalm 55) and believes the answer is to be found there:

> My heart is troubled within me: and the fear of death is fallen upon me.
>
> Fear and trembling are come upon me: and darkness hath covered me.
>
> And I said: who will give me wings like a dove, and I will fly and be at rest?
>
> Lo, I have gone far off flying away; and I abide in the wilderness.
>
> I waited for him that hath saved me from pusillanimity of spirit and a storm.

Merton writes that it is "terror that is driving me into solitude" and sees the fear as arising from the contradiction between "my nature and my God."[3] After a further incident, Merton writes:

> What exhausts me is the entertainment of all my illusions ... shaken with storms of passion and of fear ... And so I go on trying to walk on the waters of the breakdown. Worse than ever before and better than ever before ... I am aware of Him in the agony of knowing obscurely that I am paralyzed and know nothing.[4]

Merton becomes increasingly clear about the false self, "a cold house of my own devising," yet in the midst of what he describes as, "emptiness and helplessness and humiliation. Aware that I might crack up at any moment. I find, nevertheless, that when I pray, I pray better than ever." It is this breakdown that leads Merton to a new decision, to spend time in solitude as a hermit in the woods – "to keep me from folding up completely."[5]

Harry Williams[6] also suffered from anxiety, panic attacks and depression; what he calls his breakdown initially took the form of feelings of dizziness and fear: "I became more and more the victim of terror," developing increasing phobias about sitting for meals, traveling, going into a church or a shop, until, eventually, he became unable to walk outside at all, and then lost the use of his legs. One interpretation would be that he became overwhelmed, physically paralysed by all the persecutory emotions that had remained unprocessed in his unconscious mind. Following unhelpful, but well-meaning, input from a priest, a psychiatrist arranged for three weeks in a Nursing Home. Williams comments that healing from inside the church including confession, anointing with oil by the Bishop, and, continuous Holy Communion could not work, he also found that when he made no improvement his fellow clergy became angry themselves, instead accusing him of malingering "and exhorting me to pull up my socks and show some signs of a stiff upper lip." He appreciated that their inability to help felt like a threat to themselves, but, as Williams explains, the healing could not work because he recognized that "there was in myself too great a confusion between the true God and my persecuting idol." Many suppressed emotions, some childhood trauma and too much religious guilt had become pathological, and projected onto a superegoic and punishing god who commanded him to follow various rituals and behave only in certain ways. Williams describes this as being suffocatingly tedious, but worse was the suppression and reduction of his personality:

For this God of mine forbade me to be three-quarters of what

I was ... God wanted me to be an emotional dwarf so that I might give my stunted heart wholly to him ... and this meant that enjoying yourself too much was suspect ... you could enjoy yourself safely as a duty, but it could be dangerous to enjoy yourself as a pleasure.

Recounting his rage at his suffering, Williams writes about:

This paralysing terror always waiting to spring out at me at any moment; my consequent inability to concentrate on anything or enjoy anything; the inevitable isolation ... the prayers which were answered by nothing but the cruelty of an empty echo.

After some time he was able to get back to teaching, but Williams stayed away from church, saying no prayers, as religion felt too tainted:

I had had enough of God for the time being. It was an indescribable relief not to have this ghastly creature breathing with disapproval down my neck and to tell him instead to fuck off. It was the idol I was disposing of. But I wasn't at all clear about that at the time.

Years later, he came across the line by Yeats, "Hatred of God may bring the soul to God," which seemed to encapsulate what was happening to him; and so, the passage above could conclude:

For the one true God will never fuck off, however much you tell him to, while in the end the idol does, even if he remains in the wings and returns every now and then with his filthy magic.

One of the things that Williams broke through with this

dismantling of his false self and his false beliefs and false god, was the realization that if we wrap ourselves round with our self-belief and resulting self-importance then there is no room for us to be what we really are. He moved toward an increasingly open frame of mind, where gradually difference and differentiation became possible, with awareness and recognition that it is only human, even Christian, to be able to have mixed feelings. For, if we force the image of ourselves into a narrow description, then there is no spontaneity or imagination, and no surrender to God, and if we also force God into a narrow description then nothing is real, or can happen. Our talent is firmly buried under the weight of how we should be, and our connection to God is curtailed by how we think that God should be. If we step outside any of this, then there may be a fear of being punished.

Yet God has nothing to do with punishment. It was C. S. Lewis who wrote, "The door to Hell is locked from the inside."[7] Frank's punishment was, at this stage, his alienation from his true self, from God, and the pain of his loss, not just of his livelihood, but of his sense of who he was. Frank's hope lies in his therapy, and the therapist who will understand that Frank's anger was conceived in misery. His hope also lies in his contrition and the opening up of his inner heart.

There's an old story usually attributed to American Indians, of a grandparent teaching their grandchild in this way: "I have two wolves fighting in my heart. One wolf is vengeful, fearful, envious, resentful, and deceitful. The other wolf is loving, compassionate, generous, truthful, and serene." The child asks which wolf will win the fight, and the answer is "the one I feed." Yet, as has been pointed out, if we ignore the painful and the difficult it is just another way of feeding the wolf, but secretly pretending that the wolf doesn't even exist. The solution is to have knowledge about both parts of ourselves – by holding both these wolves in mind and developing our awareness of where each of them is. As Jesus hung between the penitent thief and the scoffing thief at Calvary, so Jesus tries to unite those two parts of each one of us. Our true self is an uncovering and integration of the whole of us.

Broken-hearted means that our heart is not unified – we are not of one heart and mind, but instead our inner world has been torn apart, perhaps through loss and tragedy or rage and bitterness. Darkness has taken us over, and love has been pushed to one side. It is at this point that we may feel repentance, but also to balance this we are encouraged to feel mercy. We are invited to become a Good Samaritan to ourselves. The story of the Good Samaritan allows us to appreciate all the different parts of ourselves: the wounded, half-dying, and beaten up part of ourselves, as well as the part of ourselves that represses the wounded damaged part, and the part that walks by on the other side. The part of ourselves that represses or ignores our inner world in case it becomes too much, or takes over the persona; but, there is also the part of ourselves that is potentially the rescuer as well. When I am broken-hearted and betrayed, wounded and abandoned, it is then that the Good Samaritan will once again come to meet me, and thus, show me my true identity.

> The Good Samaritan is a vision of myself. He is me with my deepest capacities no longer hedged in and constricted, but brought into play. He is me fulfilling myself by active compassion for another ... So I shall repent once more, and again be what I am.[8]

Awareness of these different parts of ourselves, allows us to expand our sense of who we are, and gives us a choice. In other words, being in a broken-hearted state can be a time of waking up, and part of the discovery can include accepting the merciful part of us. If we can help ourselves, then we will also be able to help others. The story of the Good Samaritan is a tale about power and mercy. In the telling of the parable, Jesus cuts through conventional social norms about who is deserving of help, of who is good and who is bad. The Samaritan shows mercy, and so love cuts through all classifications. If someone has to be just like me before I love them, then the person is not loved for being human, but rather for confirming me to myself – which also implies that I only love myself if I fulfill how I'm expected to be. But as Thomas Merton explains, the parable is not just about loving, it is rather about a divine revelation, and at the heart of the revelation is the idea of mercy.

> It is the faithful, the indefectible mercy of God. It is ultimate and unfailing because it is the power that binds one person to another in a covenant of hearts. It is the power that binds us to God because he has promised us mercy and will never fail in His promise.[9]

The parable shows us the mystery of power and mercy that lie at the heart of faith, because, it is in the end, also Jesus Christ himself who lies half dead, wounded and robbed by the side of the road as in the Good Friday story and yet it is Christ who comes by in the person of the Samaritan, seen as the outcast with no moral standing. Where the outcast leans down in pity to help the other:

> Then there takes place a divine epiphany and an awakening ... There reality is made human, and in answer to this movement of compassion a Presence is made on the earth ... Perhaps the encounter is outwardly sordid and unattractive. But the Presence of God is brought about on earth there, and Christ is there, and God is in communion with man.[10]

As the wounded part of ourselves is compassionately met by the outcast part, so a pattern of healing is formed which can be replicated in our encounters with others, and it is this mercy that leads us to the heart of our faith. "When I can be a person like the Good Samaritan and do what he did, then, I feel, I shall be fully me and abundantly alive."[11] The journey through betrayal, repentance, and into mercy, continues throughout our lives, and the mercy can only be taken in slowly, and in little amounts at any one time. This is why repentance is a continuous process recurring again and again, because the potential for becoming who God intends us to be is limitless. The cross of Christ can give us confidence, and it is on the basis of this confidence that we are ready to establish communion with our world. "And the more I am thus in personal relation to everything I am, the more shall I be able to afford communion with other people."[12] If I feel lovable in myself, and are no longer despising myself, then I need have no worry about relating to others and their opinion – possible adverse – of me. The story of the cross is ultimately one of transformation of broken-heartedness and agony into something life giving and life enhancing.

Chapter 6

Two Halves – One Heart

If only it were all so simple! If only there were evil people somewhere insidiously committing evil deeds, and it were necessary only to separate them from the rest of us and destroy them. But the line dividing good and evil cuts through the heart of every human being. And who is willing to destroy a piece of his own heart? During the life of any heart this line keeps changing place.[1]

Do not let your hearts be troubled, and do not let them be afraid. *John 14: 27*

Keep your heart with all vigilance, for from it flow the springs of life. *Proverbs 4: 23*

The heart is a symbol that amongst other things represents the holding of conflicting passions; a symbolic container for love and hate, and, as has been discussed in earlier chapters, for hardness and for compassion. We are indeed a mixed bag, a confusion of good and evil. Indeed, we are not good one moment and evil the next, rather, our good never seems to be entirely pure, often with mixed motives, and our badness never seems to be devoid of some good desire, regardless of how perverted and distorted that desire might seem to be. It is suggested that it is the human condition to move between opposing emotions: happiness and sadness, the good and the bad, from times of darkness to times of light and love, from times when God seems present to times when God feels absent. Yet, sometimes, one negative emotion predominates, and then it seems as if the world is all darkness, and so it becomes harder to recognize that the light will come again – that the pendulum can always swing in the other direction. For at times the world seems too cruel, when it appears that hearts dominated by brutality, meanness, strife and cold-hearted hatred have conquered; but, as we read in the gospels, what looks like the utter defeat of the crucifixion is in fact the beginning of an integration of the dark and the light to create a new dawn.

Times like this can be a real test of faith – a limbo time of dark uncertainty; a time when we can know our true dependency on God and surrender our very being into his hands. If we can hold onto God in these times then this is what has been called naked faith, a faith that is not destroyed by external events or internal emotions, but rather is a simple trust that God is with us, no matter what. Most psychotherapeutic work takes place in a state of mind a bit like Holy Saturday. The trauma has happened, and the rebirth has not yet taken place. It is a time of waiting in what feels like darkness, although, as in the darkness of the tomb, small changes and incremental shifts are beginning to happen – underneath the surface – where God's loving power is made perfect in weakness. The weakness has all to be gone through rather than swept to one side, or in some strange way reversed. The conflicts of the cross are the conflicts between mercy and brutality, generosity and meanness, peace with strife, and a loving warm-heartedness with cold-heartedness and hatred.

The most depressed and desolate place is where love is not possible. When the power of love is present, then even desperate adverse circumstances that still bring great suffering can be transformed through love. Most of us have a terribly restricted capacity to truly love which may stem from our childhood or later life experiences, but even that small capacity can be brought as an offering to God who will "raise you from your present deadness by his own creative love."[2] Once again, the cold hateful heart of stone is transformed into a warm heart of flesh, and the heart of flesh, with all its opposing emotions, is infused by divine love. Nothing is wasted, and everything that we are can meet on the cross, and be used as part of the Easter resurrection. This is why even deadness of heart includes the opportunity for a new heartbeat.

When I met with Carly again, she told me that after her Maundy Thursday experience she had decided to see a spiritual director, and that initially it had gone really well.

Carly

I went to see someone who had been recommended to me by the vicar. She's a retired clergywoman and I immediately felt safe around her, and felt able to tell her all about everything straight away. I was surprised how all sorts of things poured out ... I thought after it was like dumping a huge pile of rubbish on the floor between us. But she seemed very understanding, and I felt really sure that I wanted to believe properly in God again, and to feel closer to him, and felt that this was someone whom I could trust to help me. Let's see, right at the start she said that all God asks is that we try to be authentic and real in our relationship with him and then in our relationships with one another, and to do that we have to be authentic to ourselves. She seemed to think that I had been too compliant in the past, well she didn't make it sound like a criticism, but more something that I might want to sort out, and, she said, and I thought that this was important that our mind is a main part of our spiritual life, and God speaks to us through our thoughts and feelings, she said after all how else can he reach us? I saw her every couple of months, but I have to say it really helped, and I usually left feeling very peaceful and held in some unfamiliar way.

When I told her about the Maundy Thursday and Good Friday experiences that had started me back on the road again, she said that the message was that alongside surrender and death, there is always resurrection and new birth. I think her words were that there is a rhythm and a paradox to it which is partly why it is such a mysterious experience. And all that made me feel just so hopeful. So, it was all going really well, but ... then it must be almost a year after we started meeting she began to annoy me, and I felt that she was implying that it was time to move on and be more grown up. She seemed to have everything sorted, or at least that's what I thought, and I think I wanted to talk more about depression and how low I can feel, and she seemed to be saying I wasn't trying or something, not sure if she meant I could be more forgiving, and let it go, and that in the end it wasn't that big a deal what had happened. Actually, to tell you the truth, I've rather forgotten what she did say, or what was in my head, but anyway suddenly I felt she was no longer on my side, and didn't like me, and at that moment I really hated her and so ... oh God, it makes me all hot and bothered thinking about it but I ended up becoming sulky with her, and a bit mean and moody – like saying I didn't think it was helping anyway, and then I walked out ... I felt angry again with the church, and all the stuff I used to feel came bubbling up again.

So, I left that meeting without saying goodbye properly or arranging another time, and then I felt absolutely terrible. What I was thinking was mainly that I keep making a mess of things and so that I must be a lost cause. Deep down I could see that I had made all that happen, and that I was one of the ungrateful ones – one of those who has a chance at a relationship with God and throws it away, one of the worst sinners, just like the seed that fell on the wrong sort of soil, the feeble person given the talent who did nothing with it, or even worse one of those who called for Jesus to be crucified, and then mocked him on the cross, a betrayer. I felt my heart was broken – again – but this time there was no hope, nothing left, and it was my fault – again! I also felt I couldn't really do anything though I now think that's rubbish; for a start I could have contacted her to say sorry or asked to see her.

Anyway, in the end it did actually turn out okay ... after a few days I got an email from the spiritual director booking another time, and suggesting we might make it sooner rather than later given what had happened when we last met. I was dreading seeing her, but she was completely like before, and it seemed that she liked me again. She was kind and calm, but wanted to understand what I thought had happened, and how we might understand it as insight, and part of my recovery – "a gift from God" I think she called it! I was amazed and relieved, and she said she thought that there was a powerful critical disapproving part in me, a very unloving part she said and she linked this to what she called the punitive god – not the loving God, but one that had to be given sacrifices and placated. She thought that I was struggling to accept the loving God rather than the punitive god, and that this struggle emerged every so often as it had done when we met, when I had thought she wanted to hurt or punish me. We talked quite a bit about it all, and I felt so much better – really accepted again, and then she said the biggest battle is now to accept yourself, like God does she said. I told her that after the bad session, I had felt so awful, really grim. She asked me whether I had heard the phrase, "the dark night of the soul" – well I hadn't, but she told me it was from a fifteenth-century writer John of the Cross, who wrote a long canticle or poem which he composed during a time when he was imprisoned in a dungeon. She thought I might identify with it, because in a way I had been imprisoned – not in an external sense, but by my thoughts. It was as if the dungeon keeper which was in fact only a small part of me and my thinking, held the key to everything else and made it all feel dark and difficult.

In fact, I found a book on the canticle written by John of the Cross and his other writing and that helped me understand what the verses meant and I thought what a beautiful poem it was. I didn't really get it all, but it somehow resonated with me. One of the things that the spiritual director had suggested was that she thought it might help me if I went to a meditation group, so I've now joined one that meets once a week, for just an hour. We listen to a short talk by someone, and then meditate for about twenty minutes, and then have a tea and leave. We meet in a church hall, though it's not run by a vicar or anybody like that and it's helped me feel calmer and better inside, but also I think I now see that I can't, and, in the past wasn't able to either be in control of the world in the way that perhaps I had been expected to be, and I expected myself to be. What the spiritual director says is, that even in dark times, there is some sort of wisdom and inner guidance that can lead us in the right direction, and it's best to address it and not ignore it. The other thing is that it can just be a whole lot of little things coming together in one's mind – that's what I think happened when I was nasty to her and when I really hated her …

Carly told me quite a bit about the book she had been reading about John of the Cross[3] and explained that she and the spiritual director had also talked about it over a couple of meetings. For Carly, the negative or hateful part of herself or, using the language of the canticle, "the night" feels as if it can just come upon her and leave her feeling out of control, so it seemed to help then also seeing the night as the place of resurrection and the time of healing. Carly said how she understood that the healing couldn't be just made to happen, it happened in relationship with God. She and the spiritual director had talked about these negative feelings as part of the spiritual journey, and as included on the journey towards and with God. Carly said that one of the things she had worked out was that part of her difficulties stemmed from wanting things to be different, wanting to know God and wanting to sort it all out and be a different person, rather than staying with who she is, and opening herself to new experiences without too much expectation. She said that it was in wanting the spiritual director to really like her, and approve of her, that the difficulties began; now she felt she accepted that they were working together, and the director was alongside her, accompanying her. She said that she was trying to be honest with herself and about herself, to accept when she felt low, but to try not to define herself through being a victim, but gaining something when she felt she was suffering, which, as she added, is after all a fact of life.

John of the Cross writes how healing cannot be conjured up, we can heal ourselves superficially, but deep healing comes from God, and part of the process is in the waiting. In his writing, he describes people impatient that they want to be saints in a day:

> Many make great resolutions and plans, but as they are not humble, and have no distrust of themselves, the more resolutions they make, the further they fall, and the more annoyed they become. They do not have the patience to wait until God gives them what they seek when he so desires.[4]

In the night, in the negative and hateful part of our heart, there is still God-content; again John of the Cross encourages us to view all the struggles and difficulties of life as coming from the hand of God, for the person's good; it is healing for her and brings a great blessing:

> When you are burdened, you are joined to God. He is your strength, and he is with people who suffer. ... It is in the difficulties which test our patience that the virtue and strength of the soul [and one could add the heart] is increased and affirmed.[5]

As the spiritual writer Eckhart Tolle describes it, suffering is one of the doorways through which "presence" can occur, in other words, shaken out of our comfortable or self-satisfied view of ourselves, we are released, and awakened for the impact of God. Any reversal in our complacency can carry the coming of God, and stripping ourselves of our defenses can become what certain religious writers call a purifying experience. Importantly, it is also in the everyday and the ordinary, and in the daily round of our lives and in the boring and the mundane that change and integration can happen, through allowing the inflow of the presence of God. Another word for this is resurrection, which occurs to us as we are, often quietly and silently, and when it is least expected. When there is desolation and downheartedness life can feel a dark void, but inevitably tiny slivers of light will start to appear. John of the Cross understood this too, in the sense of both active and passive being present in the night. Where in the active night there are supernatural experiences that Iain Matthew says, "are certainly not of one's own doing"; whereas, the passive night, involves facing hardships which require our resilience. This, then, in many ways is the essence of faith, to trust even when there has been failure or betrayal, holding to the authentic when there is much falseness, "letting oneself be carried by God."[6]

This awareness of the two halves within the one heart is an acknowledgment of the inevitable mixed emotions that all humans experience, (and sometimes at the same time), and is part of what makes us human. It can feel intolerable, hence the desire to banish, especially the negative into the unconscious; however, another approach is the idea of balancing opposing feelings and states of mind, holding the hope alongside the despair, accepting "both/and" rather than "either/or." This is called holding the tension of the opposites and many believe that this leads to integration and a sense of wholeness. Carl Jung made ideas about living with the tension of the opposites, and the integration of opposing tendencies, the center of his psychological studies. He called this coincidentia oppositorum, the coincidence or meeting of opposites, meaning being aware of opposing emotions or parts of the psyche. Jung speaks about an inner cleavage – the state of being at war with oneself:

What drives people to war with themselves is the suspicion or the knowledge that they consist of two persons in opposition to one another. The conflict may be between the sensual and the spiritual man, or between the ego and the shadow. It is what Faust means when he says: "Two souls, alas, are housed within my breast."[7]

Such division happens in everyday life, and, in exceptional circumstances, where at the personal level, our thinking about ourselves and the world is often obscured by one aspect or another. It is as if the two halves of the heart are seeking to obliterate each other, instead of acknowledging that they have to function with one another for the whole heart to keep life flowing. Jung calls the healing and inner reconciliation needed to balance the opposites a religious problem.

Jung thought that it was only by appreciating the opposite feelings in one's mind, and indeed in the world, that one could have a sense of wholeness, but doing so in an authentic way is difficult. He referred to the thinking of the philosopher Meister Eckhart on this who saw a coincidence of opposites between God and man, the divine and the human, and who sought to unite the opposites by discovering God within his own soul; a task which also occupied Jung himself. Jung also quoted the medieval theologian Nicholas of Cusa, who saw the coincidence of opposites as a way of knowing God if the contradiction between opposites can be acknowledged and then surpassed. Cusa writes:

When I am at the door of the coincidence of opposites, guarded by the angel stationed at the entrance of paradise, I begin to see you, O Lord. For you are where speaking, seeing, hearing, tasting, touching, reasoning, knowing and understanding are the same and where seeing coincides with being seen, hearing with being heard, tasting with being tasted, touching with being touched, speaking with hearing, and creating with speaking.[8]

Cusa's idea of the meeting of the opposites is also summed up in his phrase "learned ignorance," where the highest knowledge is to know that one is ignorant.[9] If we are not limited by the need to know and pin everything down, then there is the opportunity to reach beyond where both knowing and not knowing meet. Cusa locates the coincidence of opposites within a divine simplicity where God enfolds us. There, all things coincide, but God is beyond such difference. Jung thought that as we grow older through the very act of living, we are forced to come to terms with contradictions, and through recognizing, experiencing, and integrating such experiences, we move closer to God and to the true self.

Thomas Merton also thought that the true self is there where we experience opposing feelings and reach to unite them through God. This feeling of transcendence is sometimes granted in glimpses, intimations that take us *beyond* the conflict, where there is an experience of unity transcending all the distinctions and differentiations. This is a creative act, and a breaking through to eternity, where we reach out to what is higher than our self. Thomas Merton clearly knew only too well about the differing drives and feelings within himself; for example, yearning toward inward contemplation and at the same time prayerful concern for humanity, opposites which he largely kept in balance. He also knew about trying to unite difference within himself: "We must contain all divided worlds in ourselves and transcend them in Christ."[10] He well appreciated that there was meaning in difference. He wrote: "The real order of the cosmos is an apparent disorder, the 'conflict' of opposites which is in fact a stable and dynamic harmony."[11]

Being fully alive is about holding the experience of the ongoing struggle between the loving warm-hearted part of ourselves, and, the hating, cold-hearted or disheartened parts of ourselves. This idea of the tension of holding the opposites is not something that happens through logic or rational thought, but only through our experience of living. So, as we live, we learn to hold the intolerable and the tolerable in some sort of balance. Such a holding can often be contained in a symbol – such as the heart – unifying and so transcending the opposites; there are the two parts of the heart, but beating as one. This part of the journey takes us to wisdom, where God is the heart of the world, and the space where all opposites and contradictions are held and removed. This too is part of the mystery of creation, a mystery of the opposites and of paradox, in which God is born in a human and a human is reborn in God.

Chapter 7

Taking Heart

In the midst of winter, I found there was within me, an invincible summer. And that makes me happy. For it says no matter how hard the world pushes against me, within me there is something stronger – something better pushing right back.[1]

Hope does not disappoint us, because God's love has been poured into our hearts through the Holy Spirit that has been given to us. *Romans 5: 5*

Were not our hearts burning within us ... Luke 24: 32

Why might we take heart? In the midst of dark times, when negativity holds sway, it seems impossible to remember that "this too will pass," but the story of the crucifixion and resurrection invites us to do just that. After all, the tomb, the place of the past, the dead and the despairing is in a garden – the place of growing plants, alive to the elements, and indeed Mary mistakes Jesus for the gardener – the one who encourages green shoots and fruits. The heart of the matter is this, that change will eventually take place; after all change is the only constant. Perhaps the inevitability of change is then, without sounding too hopeful, a sign of hope, something we can take heart from.

St Paul gives us a glimpse of this in his letter to the Romans: "Now hope that is seen is not hope. For who hopes for what is seen? But if we hope for what we do not see, we wait for it with patience" (8: 22–25). Once we see what we have hoped for, it is no longer hope, but a reality. Paul explains that hope is not to be confused with optimism, but it is rather something that derives from suffering: suffering produces endurance, endurance produces character, and character produces hope (5:3–4). Here is an example of something arising from the tension of holding the opposites, and all those mixed up feelings – hopefulness; it's not a certainty as there is no guarantee, but there will be change – we can take heart.

Thomas Aquinas thought that hope is, simply put, leaning on God; he expressed it in this way: "Our hope pertains to God on whose help it leans"[2] so hope is less about us, and more about God, it becomes a leaning into dependence. Hope is then the unshakeable awareness that God *is*, and so this is clearly linked to faith and the belief in love. The Dominican priest Donald Goergen, who quotes Aquinas, believes that ultimately our hope is for things to get better, and linked to this is forgiveness; he speaks about the cup at the Last Supper and then at the Eucharist as a sign of our solidarity with both the hope and the suffering of the world. In the prophetic tradition, the cup can be one of blessing and salvation (Ps 116: 13 and Ps 16: 5) or a cup of suffering (Jeremiah 49: 12). The cup of suffering is often not a cup from which one wants to drink. The question that Jesus asks is haunting: Are you able to drink the cup that I drink? Perhaps, we feel that as Christians, especially those of us living in the so-called first world, we are privileged, and so we ought to be spared the cup at the same time that we are able to drink from it. In other words, we have the sense that we are entitled to a kind of hope denied to most of the rest of the world, where daily life can be a struggle and the hope is to survive. Given this privileged status, Goergen thinks that our ultimate hope lies in forgiveness. That is collective hope for a change in the world, and there is also personal hope for ourselves which happens at many levels.

Hope changes as our circumstances change, and what we hope for today may not be the same as what we hope for tomorrow, hope manifests in different ways but we cannot live without it and with it comes wholeness. This is shown in the story of *The Death of Ivan Ilyich* by Leo Tolstoy[3] when Ilyich in his final illness is swinging between false hope that he will recover, and the despair that he will not, and, so, is only able, to know true hope when he is able to acknowledge the truth to himself, namely that he has squandered his life on what was unimportant, with this realization he can then discover the real thing in life:

> Just then his son crept quietly into the room and went up to his bed. The dying man was still screaming desperately and flailing his arms. One hand fell on the boy's head. The boy grasped it, pressed it to his lips, and began to cry. At that very moment Ivan Ilyich fell through and saw a light, and it was revealed to him that his life had not been what it should have but that he could still rectify the situation. "But what is the real thing?" he asked himself and grew quiet, listening. Just then he felt someone kissing his hand. He opened his eyes and looked at his son.
>
> Ilyich had discovered what was important in life – the real thing.

I wasn't able to meet with Helen again for quite some time – several years after our last discussion, when Helen was finding out from her work with the children's classes about her inner world with all its complexities. Helen looked different when we met again, quite frail, and explained that she had been ill, and that it had taken a good six months to recover, and she still had to limit her activities – for a start no more work with the children. This loss in her ability to keep busy and to go out had initially left her feeling a bit low and hopeless.

Helen
I'm actually a lot more optimistic than I was a few months ago, as I understand that I will feel better in due course, but I'm also reluctant to be as busy as I was before, as I think that in part led to the illness developing, and also I've lost a

lot of energy. It means that Roger now has to do more which isn't great for him, and I suppose for the first time I've been feeling my age. I think I need to make some changes to my life, and to find what's most important and stick with that ... obviously family and friends, and keeping the house and garden going, but I've also been able to take heart from the fact that I do have some more time for religion – not the being on committees sort of religion, but something that is more about what is going on inside me and what I really believe. When I felt physically so poorly, I was in bed for about three weeks as I just couldn't get out of bed ... I wondered if I was going to die. That, I can tell you, focused my mind. And now I'm a lot better, but I realize that because of my age I'm drawing closer to the end of my life, so it has made me think that it's time for some changes to be made, and not just on the surface ... like stopping doing the children's classes and that sort of thing ... but something more. And I can see that that's somehow my responsibility, I'm going to make some decisions. You see, lying in bed, I found myself wondering about my life, thinking "was that it?" Okay, I worked for a while in a bank, and then I married Roger, and in those days you didn't really go back to work once you had children, so I was more or less at home, though loving looking after my girls, then I thought I might train as a teacher, but then my son turned up – an afterthought, but a very welcome one, so I put all those plans on hold ... and once they had grown up, I went back to work for a while doing some admin in a local firm ... just part time, but it was a way of getting out of the house and I enjoyed it. Then there were the grandchildren – coming for visits, and one of my daughters lives quite near so we helped with her children, but they're all teenagers now or grown up so they're less interested in coming over, and they're busy with their own lives anyway. I've kept busy all my life, doing things and trying to make things all right for those around me.

Still, I've been saying to myself now there is another side to life, and it's not just about going to church – religion I mean – I know there's more to it, but although I want to discover whatever it is, I'm also stalling on making any changes. It's silly really; I'm talking about it not just in my head, but to other people too, but then not really doing anything about it. But I am by nature quite a hopeful person, so I am thinking that something will turn up one of these days; in the meantime I'm reading a few bits and pieces ... the vicar has a couple of shelves of books at church – well it's in the church hall, quite a nice little library really, and people donate books on religion, so I'm having a look there every so often. At the moment I'm using a book of daily readings, so I'm taking a bit of time to read that through each day, and actually getting quite a lot out of some of them – I don't understand them all, but last week there was a wonderful one, I really thought that it had been written for me ... it was just what I was feeling ... let me read a bit of it to you: "we are really completely in God's hands and that, with all our incapacity, we can serve Him very well by staying there and responding to what our times ask of us, insofar as we can."[4] And, in fact, a couple of days later, the words seemed to hit me again, listen to this:

"My life is in many ways simple, but it is also a mystery which I do not attempt to really understand, as though I were led by the hand in a night where I see nothing, but can fully depend on the Love and Protection of Him Who guides me."

The vicar has been to visit a few times, and we've actually had a good talk about faith, and I think I'm beginning to get a sense of letting go and having to trust God ... I know I said earlier about it being my responsibility to make changes, but the truth is, I am being forced to be more passive, and so now I think I mean more that if something comes along then I need to respond, but I don't yet know what that might be, so at the moment I'm sticking with the reading, and thinking about stuff. The other thing I've been reading is poetry. First of all I went back to William Wordsworth which in fact we studied at school, but I found I was remembering it, and Roger bought me a general anthology so I'm dipping in and out of poems most days. It's quite restful and inspiring too. In the anthology I came across a poem by Philip Larkin called "Church Going" which of course caught my attention, and in particular one line – let's see if I can find it. Yes, I have it in my notebook which I'm now keeping to jot things down that take my fancy: "A hunger in himself to be more serious." I thought having been ill, there's now a hunger in myself to be more serious. It's probably the last chance I have ... So, really, in a way perhaps I'm just seeing what's going to happen, as I don't really know what else to do, but perhaps that sounds rather passive, but I'm hopeful, and I think I now feel that I have a deeper faith than I had before – well it feels more personal and so I think that there's an opportunity for finding meaning, so I'm taking heart from that.

Helen's illness had forced change upon her and her lifestyle, but she was also open to inner change, which is not so much about purposively moving from A to B or stopping one thing and taking up another, but is rather an experience of gradual transformation. The change that Helen is looking for is already happening, but more as a spiral process, where one thing may lead to another, and is well described by James Alison as starting off, taking wrong directions, getting lost, getting very lost, being found, new life, and losing oneself. Spiritual transformation involves an increasing consciousness of God at the center: "it is the sense that the real subject of the universe, the world, and of my life, is God."[5]

So, what is this experience of God that is found in spiritual transformation? Here we can turn as Carly did to John of the

Cross, who, in his own searching in the dark night for a God whom he felt was hidden, was able to open up what such an experience might be.[6] As Iain Matthew writes, John of the Cross is looking for encounter – not a feeling of encounter but a person. The dilemma is that God is beyond us and "other." "God remains to be named when we have named all that can be named." "Of God himself," John writes, "nothing could be said that would be like him." Despite this transcendent God, we, like John of the Cross, long for an immanent encounter, and this can only be sought in faith and love. John clearly states: "The more faith the soul has, the more she is united with God," and "the more hope the soul has, the greater her union with God." John's message is to believe in the God who has revealed himself in Jesus Christ – that is the experience, and that is the real event. So, to live in faith and hope, "even though it be in darkness, since in this darkness it is God who supports the soul. Cast your care on God, since he has care of you. He won't forget you."

Jim Forest puts it like this,

It is after all Christ's truth that matters, a truth we experience from time to time but which can never be adequately expressed in words or be obtained by movements and causes. Trying to live within Christ's truth certainly doesn't mean we live an undented life, a life free from disappointments, but it may help prevent disappointment from becoming despair.[7]

This is like Helen's letting go, living a life that has been dented and is not free from disappointment, but in accepting that there is nothing much that can be done actively, there is a desire to make room, and invite in the God who longs to befriend us. It is about making room for God in order to receive. Something will then take place which is bigger than the person, and that is: "faith is God lifting the soul into God's own life" – it comes from God, and leads to God. This is grace which is the indwelling of

God in the person, and the person sharing the life of God faith-hope-love. Perhaps it is this coming to know that one is known, or as St Paul describes it: "you have come to know God, or rather to be known by God" (Galatians 4: 9) and again (Corinthians 1, 8: 3) "anyone who loves God is known by him." James Alison describes this experience in this way: "And this 'being known' is in fact the reception of a loving regard towards which we, like so many heliotropes, find ourselves empowered to stretch in faith and hope." Faith and hope is then the response within us which is called forth by love: "relaxing into love's discovery of us."[8]

Awakening to the mystery of being can only really happen when we have an opportunity to see beyond our own needs, troubles, and desires. As Helen reflects on poetry and the daily readings, she has begun to discover the reality of "the Being" beyond her previous everyday being. And in her responses to what she is reading, to have a glimpse that this Being is personal, and can speak to her through anything or anyone and at any time. This is the beginnings of feeling known by God and the beginnings of contemplation.

In his account of a meditation workshop, Chris MacKenna describes how it is really possible to set aside expectations, and, as far as possible, our projections so as to open ourselves and contemplate:

The leader placed a raisin in the palm of each participant's hand. It felt like Holy Communion. For several minutes we were encouraged to examine the raisin, to study its creases, roll it around, absorb its color, texture and smell. Then we were invited to hold it in our mouths, explore it with our tongues, and register its taste and feel, before biting into it, chewing, and swallowing ... in the five or so minutes taken by the exercise, the atmosphere in the room changed and became numinous. Afterwards we were reluctant to break the silence.[9]

Here was transformation – not just to the raisin, but with the members of the workshop, and to the world around them, and as MacKenna adds,

> to the mystery of Being which enfolds and confronts us ... the Bible uses impersonal, as well as personal imagery to evoke the experience of God: God as fire, rock, water, shade. It is as if everything partakes of the reality of God's being, and yet no-thing and no-person can be equated with the mysteries of God.

An exercise like that gives a glimpse into what it can be like to really look and see something, or indeed somebody, as it is or as they are, and without imposing our own thoughts and feelings. This is then the beginning of contemplation – developing the ability to be, and to allow the other to be as well, because if one can recognize the reality of the other, there is free space in which religious transformation can take place. So, can we allow God into this space too? And if we do, what does this mean? This would be a space where God is neither literally a religious object out there, a figure to be worshiped and praised (though there is that aspect too), nor, nothing but a projection of our inner world (though there may be aspects of that remaining too). Instead, this is then predominantly a transitional space, where we can wonder about our spiritual experiences using imagination, metaphor, myth, story, poetry and music. God then becomes transformational, acting as a processor known through continuous action that alters our very being – helping us to become the people that God has intended us to be. This transformational action occurring in our inmost parts is about relationship, a relationship through which our true self can be articulated, recognized and welcomed. This is not "out there" change, but "in here" change and the change is itself that of God. Thomas Merton expresses this idea of inner change and transformation in a way that Helen might resonate with, when Merton writes towards the end of his own life:

There is a need of effort, deepening, change and transformation. Not that I must undertake a special project of self-transformation or that I must "work on myself." In that regard it would be better to forget it. Just to go for walks, live in peace, let change come quietly and invisibly on the inside.[10]

But he also understood that this is a process involving ourselves with God, and our part includes the desire to make changes, and to be serious in our attempts, he continues:

But I do have a past to break with, an accumulation of inertia, waste, wrong, foolishness, rot, junk, a great deal of clarification of mindfulness, or rather of no-mind – a return to genuine practice, right effort, need to push onto the great doubt. Need for the Spirit.

Hang on to the clear light!

Experiences of transformation require our radical passivity, which is our participation through some lowering of our resistances, and our defenses – which can happen when we are vulnerable or ill, if only to the extent that we can perceive what is happening to us. Our passivity in the context of God's creativity becomes radical, when we stop seeing God as a threat to our sense of self. It is not to do with our attitude or behavior, or being lazy or indolent, but to do with our very self – created by and for God. As the monk Sebastien Moore writes, "How could the creative act of God threaten us, since it constitutes us? Truly to know myself is to know that I am, in and for my very existence, 'known of God,' passive."[11] This passivity has been likened to the child mind, which is about those sorts of moments when we are completely present and open, trusting – a radical passivity. It is a sense of being taken out of ourselves, surprised by some consciousness of the light, or a change of consciousness, with the restoration of moments of deep connection and renewal. It is about a process of developing and becoming – it is about closeness to God. This presence and passivity to what is within and around us, is a state we all knew in infancy before conceptual thought began to obscure and confuse us, but it can be re-found – often through times of letting go and contemplation. As adults then this is something of the past, but, interwoven with adult experience and from the synthesis of the two apparently opposite states of mind something new emerges. Thomas Merton describes it as innocence – experience – innocence. William Blake, the poet and visionary, wrote about something very similar which was the synthesis of innocence and experience leading to what he called organized innocence.[12]

Radical passivity is very vulnerable, trusting, and defenseless, but it is held within the adult consciousness and perception. Radical passivity is the source of endless growth, "the wellspring of eternal flourishing."[13] It enables us to take heart, because, if we can let go, and let God act within us, we might find that we are already known and held in God. This process allows us to see the false self or the mask that we have been wearing as a way of protecting our real being, the true self – the person that God intends us to be. As our true self shyly emerges, so all parts of us become affected, and it is this that feels like rebirth because we are being transformed. Therefore, we can take heart, because faith, hope and love transform our self through God's action from within. If we allow this to happen then God can change us and recreate us without displacing us and this action within our radical passivity, our surrender and receptivity to love, is gradually allowing us "to become someone."[14] All experience changes us and changes the self; however, some experiences transform us to a greater depth than others. As Carl Jung says,

> In the end the only events in my life worth telling are those when the imperishable world irrupted into this transitory one. That is why I speak chiefly of inner experiences ... All other memories ... have paled into insignificance.[15]

It is the gradual awareness that leads us to realize that change and transformation has happened, and this is then a glimpse of our salvation.

> Salvation looks like ... the perception of a hugely powerful loving project as having come toward us and caught us unawares ... In other words we thought we were in control, but we weren't. When this change begins then we finally realize that in order to come into our lives God must have really known and liked us all along.[16]

Chapter 8

A Change of Heart

For the human heart and mind are deep. *Psalm 64: 6*

Keep your heart with all vigilance, for from it flow springs of life. *Proverbs 4: 23*

Little children, let us love, not in word or speech, but in truth and action. And by this we will know that we are from the truth and will reassure our hearts before him whenever our hearts condemn us; for God is greater than our hearts, and he knows everything. *1 John 3: 18–20*

The word metanoia is used to define a transformative change of heart, and, especially, spiritual conversion. For all of us at some point in our lives there are moments where we are called to authentic personhood, often when there is some recognition of the space between the self one is and the self one could be, and at that moment we feel called to a change of heart from within ourselves. The psychoanalyst Neville Symington offers us an example of this level of change coming from within the person.[1] He describes an experience from his work when he was interested in how some people who were drug addicts, or recidivist prisoners, recovered from their condition, and got better. He writes how he had come across a fellow who had been a serious alcoholic, in and out of prison but seemingly against all odds had completely recovered. "I asked him one day … what it was that had brought about the change." The man had described how he had begun drinking again, had been thrown out by his wife and was about to be thrown out of a treatment program:

He said to himself, "There are only two things I can do: Either I commit suicide, or I take this bottle and throw it through the windows [of the alcoholic ward]." He was sitting there with rain pouring down, and he said that suddenly a very strange thought came to him. He said to himself, "Or I could decide to get better."

Symington says that the third thing-like thought was a decision, the first two weren't decisions, they were just old habits, and the new thought came unexpectedly. The difference in the third thought, and the reason it could be described as a decision, was that it was a creative thought, a moral thought, an aware thought, closely related to conscience and so a spiritual thought. What does that mean? A creative thought is one generated from within, in that sense it comes from the authentic part of the person – in other words, it's not just a thought born out of previous and restrictive experience, nor is it an ingested and repeated thought that has been communicated by others. It comes from awareness, a knowing from within that has the potential to emerge, and so to change us. In order that creativity and conscience might operate, we need to be able to make our own judgments, and not ascribe the power to another. While the actual moment of decision cannot ever be pinned down, or is it necessarily understandable why it should have happened at that particular point of time, the resulting change can be experienced and felt.

Conversion or metanoia can then be understood as a kind of movement into a new horizon that entails an about-face. It comes out of the old by repudiating characteristic features of the old, and may set one's life on a different course towards something new. The theologian Bernard Lonergan distinguishes between a horizontal conversion where there is so to speak a change of content within one's fundamental horizon, in other words new answers to old questions, and a vertical conversion where there are radically new questions that creatively restructure content into a totally new horizon.[2]

This is an ever deepening withdrawal from ignoring the realm of transcendence in which God is known and loved, and going toward an ever deeper entrance into that realm; the emphasis here is on an inner shifting, and a movement from self-absorption or self-enclosure towards self-transcendence. It is a move towards the "more than ourselves." This conversion, then, is a process that frees one from the self-enclosure that Lonergan calls radical lovelessness, because it is an awareness of the twofold process of being loved unconditionally, and responding to that radical gift by cooperating in the process whereby one's own loving becomes unconditional. It is a change of heart *from* lovelessness *to* being in love.

It seems then that one of the ways that self-transcendence happens is in the reaching out to others, and Stuart was able to speak to me about his experiences of this. When I met up with him again, he said that initially he hadn't really got anywhere much with his searching for God and meaning in a formal kind of way; in fact it had all been rather low key and negative, so about a year ago he had decided to put an effort in and he had begun going to the public library several mornings a week to read up about philosophy and religion. The library didn't open until 9.30 so there tended to be a little group of them waiting outside.

Stuart

Initially I didn't take much notice of who else was there, except seeing that we were a motley crew. There were about six or eight of us, some looked like they were what my old mum would have called "gentlemen of the road," perhaps hoping to find somewhere warm to pass the day, and a couple of us with our laptops probably going to do research, and the odd foreign student. I tended to have a coffee first, and wait at a little table – that's possible because the library entrance is inside a shopping podium where there's a café and tables and chairs. One day, this man sitting at the table next to me, said hello. I could see he was a bit odd, and my immediate response was to look away, and perhaps ignore him, but he persisted, and was asking me what I was doing on my laptop and what I was going to the library for. He seemed to have some sort of physical problems, and his speech was sometimes difficult to understand, but I wondered if he had mental health or slight learning difficulties too, and I know this is dreadful to confess, but I was relieved when the doors opened and I went down the far end to avoid him. But he was there each time I went to the library, smiling, and saying "'hello," and one day I thought what a mean bastard I was and bought him a tea – he didn't drink coffee he told me. So, strange as it may sound we got into a routine. I'd buy him a drink, and he, his name is Barry, joined me at the table and we talked about this and that. He's got his own accommodation, but isn't able to work, so likes spending time in the library looking at art books and magazines. He's actually an interesting guy and good to talk with.

Then one day Barry wasn't there, and I found I was a bit worried. Anyway he turned up the following week and told me that he had had some sort of trouble with his benefits, and brought a load of paperwork which he asked me to read and give him my opinion about what it all meant. To tell you the truth, I had a job trying to understand what had happened, but could see there had been a mix up with his payments which hadn't come through. Long story short, the problem was eventually solved, though I could see how vulnerable someone like Barry is to bureaucratic mess ups. But if this doesn't sound too patronizing, I've learnt a bit about myself, and also quite a bit from Barry. And I really like him. He's amazingly philosophical – perhaps a bit too much in the sense that he just seems to accept what life throws at him, and he's had quite a bit thrown at him over the years. The other thing is that he's so open, and finds pleasure in the smallest of things and that's made me feel like an over-privileged idiot ... searching for the meaning of life and God and ... there's Barry really happy with a tea and a bun, or when the sun shines, or he finds a good art book to look at. It's made me really think, and that's one of the things that my friendship with Barry gives me – and I do say friendship because it is mutual. And unlike other friends I have, it has in a strange sort of way helped with my searching ... as now I see it's more about just being who you are, and being able to see what's going on.

The thing is, once I gathered that, I thought I'd go on a day course on mindfulness which was helpful, I'm trying to be a bit more aware, and sometimes also slow right down and trying to be present with what I'm doing, and then a couple of months ago I found a meditation group that I'm going to regularly. It's being run in the town where I live, and it's on once a week for about half an hour. There's no real teaching though sometimes someone reads a poem, or there's a short talk or some music, and then we all meditate together. You can stay on for a tea or coffee afterwards if you feel like it, but that's just an option. It's very low key, and there's no pressure, no dogma and no expectations but I have to say it's begun to feel like something that I want and need to do. Well so much so that I've begun doing a bit of meditation each day at home. If I can do it in the mornings when I feel fresh, and before I start whatever it is I'm doing that day then that's better, but sometimes I do it in the evenings if there isn't time in the morning – the thing is, now if I don't do it for a day or two, I start to really miss it and feel restless, and well almost unhappy. There's all sorts of techniques to do with breathing, or having a word or phrase that you repeat, and I must say

I've tried to vary what I do, but mainly I do follow the breath as I breathe in and then follow it as I breathe out, and try to feel this as light coming into my body. Sometimes I count the breath, and then start again every time I realize that I have been distracted and starting thinking about other things ... which by the way is pretty often ... I like the teaching, which is that it is just one breath and if you mess up it doesn't matter – you just start over again.

I've found it's really all about paying attention. Funnily enough years ago I did a course on Buddhist meditation so I remember quite a bit from that, so it's not entirely strange. I think what I've found has happened is that I'm paying clearer attention to what I am experiencing, and my responses to whatever it is, and then somehow or other I'm able to observe them without judging myself. I think one of the things I've noticed is my wish to pin things down and to get the answers, but meditation is teaching me to keep open to all possibilities. It feels like another way of praying, but this time without all those words. It's really about emptying my mind, and waiting to see what happens. I think rather than thinking I've got to find what God is about and I've got to do it soon before I die, I'm relaxing a bit and learning to live more in the moment – after all as they say – what else is there! So, to come back to Barry, what I've found from him is this present moment thing, and that's really helped me with meditation. In some strange way, both the meditation group and having a cup of tea with Barry, take me out of myself, I forget myself, and I don't feel self-conscious. That's not to say that I didn't feel self-conscious at first in the group, especially if I managed a few moments without any thoughts coming into my head then I'd think "I'm meditating" and blow me I would have lost the moment and be back in myself again. But, gradually, I've let that go and that has been a relief. So what with one thing and another, I feel I've also relaxed my conscious searching because in an even odder way I feel I've been found or anyway found something. I've found out quite a bit about myself – prejudices and good parts both through my friendship with Barry and also in the group. They're not huge insights, but I feel more at home with myself, and so I'm not out looking for something else. It's been odd, but I feel I'm changing.

As Stuart found, one of the knock-on effects of such a change of heart is that everything else is placed in the light and also the shadow of transcendent value, suddenly *this* is what is important rather than the old ways of seeing the world, and so then the whole universe seems to be a friendlier place. There's still the good and the bad, but the seeing takes place from a different perspective. The world is then experienced holistically as the expression and manifestation of God's benevolence and beneficence: God's glory. The power of God's love brings forth a new energy and efficacy, and the limit of human expectation ceases to be the grave – there is more than the prison of the small self with all its fluctuating moods and happenings. The centrality of "I" is displaced as we discover love for another. The mystics, the solitaries, and the contemplatives of all religious traditions write of the same process which is the relinquishing of what the contemporary spiritual writer Eckhart Tolle refers to as the little me – the little me with my little past, and my little future, and while Tolle does not diminish our individual stories and sufferings, he rather places them in a wider and connected context where they assume a different proportion. Merton describes it in this way,

> Inside me, I quickly come to the barrier, the limit of what I am, beyond which I cannot go by myself. It is such a narrow limit and yet for years I thought it was the universe ... How quickly my limits accuse me of my nothingness and I cannot

go beyond. I pause and reflect and reflection makes it more final. Then I forget to reflect any more and by surprise I make a little escape, at least to the threshold, and love moves in the darkness, just enough to tell me there is such a thing as freedom.[3]

This change of heart means a change in how we experience ourselves in the world, and indeed the world itself. For the real work of conversion is a gradual turning away from our self-interest, to allow space for the unexpected reality of God. This change of heart, the conversion, and the process of continuous ongoing conversion, is a form of rebirth, a resurrection: continuous and ever deepening. The encounter awakens something in the depth of our being; something we did not know was there. This is then resurrection to liberation, power and hope. Thomas Merton adds that it's also about a capacity and resilience in life to bounce back to change, and creatively transform ourselves, even although we might feel defeated, and despite the battle between death and life that goes on within us all.

In my last meeting with Frank he had talked about the after effects of the incident at work and his feelings of guilt and depression; some months after this he sent me an email telling me of a very worrying time following his son's bike accident. This is an extract from our correspondence:

Frank
My wife and I are still in a state of shock but also very grateful because it could all have been so much worse; he is going to be all right! It was pretty bad when we got the news but the emergency services were brilliant, and everyone very kind. Basically Leo [Frank's son] went into a skid going around the corner near our house. He was on a bike, and it was raining so the road was slippery, and I guess he was going too fast – once he's home I shall let him know what I think of that,

but for now I'm overwhelmed by a feeling I haven't known before which is a deep love and tenderness for him. He's a grown lad, well seventeen so perhaps this sounds a bit odd, but seeing Leo in the hospital bed all strapped up with bits of him broken and in pain, I just felt pure love for him.

The reason that I thought I'd write to you is to say that it has put everything else in proportion – this is about life and death, and it's reminded us both how lucky we are to be alive, and for Leo to be all right, and how our life hangs on a thread ... if a car had been coming or Leo had lost his helmet – it doesn't bear thinking about except I *have* been thinking about it, and I see that once we'd recovered from the initial news there's been a change in all of us. We're all being kinder to one another. Now I know it won't necessarily last, but there's a love there between the three of us which is strong. It's helping us all through. And concentrating on Leo and his recovery is what matters now.

Frank was describing a resurrection; not just that his son was going to recover, but also a shift in the family relationships which hadn't always been easy. He was wise enough to see that this state might not last, and that there would be challenges ahead, but that in these circumstances it was love that was the powerful force; it was love that ultimately mattered. This is ordinary resurrection which we all share in, not as Merton says because we are religious heroes, but rather because we are "suffering and struggling human beings" exposed to the cross.[4] For Merton, resurrection is not a religious doctrine, but rather a way of living, where the living Christ "is risen" and is going ahead before us. And where is He going? Well, to Galilee which is the place where the past can be recovered in such a way as to make it the foundation for a new and extended identity. Rowan Williams sees Galilee as "the soil on which a redeemed future may grow,"[5] and where Galilee becomes the place of discipleship.

And the path that leads from Galilee to Jerusalem is the path towards the place of suffering and death, but also Jerusalem as the place of divine self-revelation. Merton understands that if we are to meet with Jesus in Galilee, then it is not necessarily some glorious trouble-free existence, but rather an existence perhaps permanently characterized by human failure.

Thomas Merton[6] understood this as the same mystery that is found in the Eucharist each time we participate when we die with Christ, we rise with him and receive from him the spirit of promise who transforms us and unites us to the Father in and through the Son. In this sense the renewal of the self through a change of heart is "a central fact of Christian existence," and "fundamental to Christian theology and practice." This, Merton writes is not merely a ritual affair or result of exterior acts, it is rather an inner revolution involving complete self-transcendence and transcendence of the usual cultural norms and attitudes, where all are seen as created, redeemed and loved – one in Christ. The insistent voice which urges us to search and to change, telling us, "you must be born again," is in part about a recovery of something and some quality of being that is still deep within us: it is to become ourselves. Merton saw this as the search for inner truth, and as an inner transformation of consciousness, and importantly as both a psychological and spiritual rebirth, and it is this that is the goal of authentic maturity.

> Emphasis is placed on the call to fulfill certain obscure yet urgent potentialities in the ground of one's being, to "become someone" that one already (potentially) is, the person one is truly meant to be.

Any creative change involves destruction; rebirth involves a death, and so the dynamic of continuous conversion is an earthly transformational pattern of dying and rising. The Franciscan Richard Rohr says that we need to deeply trust this pattern, and if we do we are indestructible. Rather than the death and resurrection of Jesus as some kind of heavenly transaction it is instead an earthly transformation on his and our part that can only be achieved by deep trust, but, that, in the end, saves us from meaninglessness, cynicism, hatred and violence – which is indeed death. For it seems as if the process is not one of ascent, but rather descent, and this involves going into the darkness to see the light. This it seems is what is required, and through it we will be known. The open mind and the open heart, and the willingness to think, feel, and accept what we are – it is only through such openness that our salvation can be worked out, though often with fear. The resurrection is fueled by love – the real love of God, and love of one another, and so this change of heart over time becomes the heart's orientation, an attitude learned from our encounters with the risen Lord.

Chapter 9

Getting to the Heart of It

Blessed are the pure in heart, for they will see God. *Matthew 5: 8*

Bear in mind that for cleaning your heart from sins you will obtain an infinite reward – you will see your God, your most gracious creator, your providence. *St John of Kronstadt*

The stories of Carly, Frank, Helen and Stuart all demonstrate that spiritual development and psychological change go hand in hand. Each of them has described an increasing psycho-spiritual capacity to think about emotional experiences, to allow for new developments and to open to the creative elaboration of new meanings in relationship with other people and with God. In this way the movement towards God is about "becoming"; we start to become the person that we are meant to be. I spoke to Frank nearly two years on from our last face-to-face conversation, and heard about his psychological and spiritual changes.

Frank
Well most importantly Leo has completely recovered but that deeper relationship between him and me has lasted; we're good mates now. He's in college – no more bikes I'm relieved to say. But the whole thing was another wakeup call – though now basically I think I just want a quiet life!

And as for me, it's all taken a long time, much too long, but I feel that I have changed, and can see that the whole experience of the incident at the day center, and then leaving the work that I thought I had been "called" to do affected me a great deal. I got help as you know from a therapist, and I'm still seeing him as it's a complicated business and I still sometimes feel bad about the image I had cultivated for myself, and how false that was. I guess I feel more real, even if parts of being the real me aren't so nice. But I now see it's better to be real than pretend to be something I'm not. And I am certainly more real, kinder too in the family and I think we're all happier for it.

My faith has also helped; finally I've got that together a bit more. I know I said I was ashamed to talk to the vicar, and so after a while I started going to services again, but this time I decided to keep it all low key and so went to the Cathedral in the nearby town where I could just be present without anyone needing to talk to me or chat or ask me to do things. My wife has been wonderful and supportive, and now she comes with me, but it's helpful because the place is big and we can be anonymous. I think I needed a sense of healing, I needed to get a sense of being at peace with myself and well it's a gradual process, but it's a lot better than it was. The thing is I do feel angry about stuff, but I'm able to use the anger more constructively – in fact it also makes me feel more alive, so I try to use the energy I feel to make changes – but it's all small steps at a time. In a funny sort of way I feel as if my heart is changing, as if I'm being reborn, as if I'm becoming a more true me. Time and humility have helped me heal and begin to get to the heart of who I am.

The theologian Roberta E. Bondi writes of her similar experiences in this way.[1] She describes one afternoon when overwhelmed by despair and the feelings she had failed as the mother she wanted to be and "the wife, daughter, friend, niece, historian, and teacher I had intended to be as well. The memory of all my unmet obligations ... I cried out to God ... I give up. I absolutely give up." She writes that she did give up, utterly:

My heart was torn in half, and out of these halves ran all the unmet and conflicting expectations, good intentions, and desires to please I had ever had. I didn't care if I was a good mother or a good teacher or a good daughter. I no longer suffered with those who suffered. I did not feel guilty. I did not accept my unhappiness as my due, nor did I reject it. I did not fight against what was happening to me. Emptied at last of everything, I finally felt nothing. I simply sank like a dead body into darkness.

She does not know how long she sat there, whether for a long time or just a moment, but without any warning she woke up:

I heard my own voice repeating in my mind the words from the Roman Catholic Eucharistic prayers for Easter, "The joy of the Resurrection renews the whole world." Every cell of my body heard them and for the first time I knew that these words were absolutely true, and that they were true for me. "The joy of the Resurrection renews the whole world," I repeated to myself in wonder, and while I spoke, my long-broken heart was healed ... my heart filled up with a joy so fierce that it spilled out and ran through the whole of my body and flickered around me like a flame.

What Bondi realized was that she had focused on the suffering on the cross, and the death of Jesus, rather than the life and joy it does and can bring. From this new place of self-realization, she could see that life is upheld not by pleasing others, or behaving in certain ways, nor by taking on the sufferings of others – all false ways of living based on oughts and shoulds and cemented by propaganda much of it often preached from the pulpit. Instead, her breakthrough got to the heart of it, which is that it is not through our efforts but rather God who holds all things, all living things in existence, and all and every heart is upheld by God's, "own joyous self, mysteriously, by a love so strong, so supple, and so subtle I could hardly imagine it." Bondi writing about her spiritual journey, quotes from Psalm 84 that, "On my way to Jerusalem I had at last found that the Bitter Valley of my life had become a place of springs." And, once the intensity of her breakthrough had subsided, she took up what she had been doing before but "I enjoyed all these everyday tasks with a single heart."

The promise of God's story, the promise of the scriptures, and at least the implicit promise of many mystics and spiritual seekers is that at the heart of it *in* God all things are finally healed. As Julian of Norwich expressed it, "All shall be well, and all shall be well and all manner of thing shall be well."[2] This healing of our hearts may not be in the way that we have expected, and letting go of our need to control what form this *ought* to take offers a freedom for the truly creative to emerge. This is the healing that holds all the different parts of us together; it is not that the differences become canceled out, but rather that they can be held in balance and so transcended. By overcoming the divisions within our heart we arrive at purity of heart. The biblical basis for this is in the Beatitude: "Blessed are the pure in heart, for they will see God" (Matthew 5:8); while the monastic basis is found in the spiritual searching of the desert fathers and mothers. They were searching for detachment through simplicity and clarity of vision. Thomas Merton describes it in this way: "a clear unobstructed vision of the true state of affairs, an intuitive grasp of one's own inner reality as anchored, or rather lost, in God through Christ."[3] Merton also understood that what was felt to be bad in us, the things that we do not like, still has to be integrated into our whole being.

In a talk to the monastic community at the Abbey of Gethsemani, Merton draws on the work of Isaac of Stella, a twelfth-century monk, philosopher and theologian who based his views, what we would now call his psychological insights, on the realistic idea of what a human's life is like and the dynamism involved. His thinking here is that there is nothing in us that is evil in itself, but the evil in us comes from something good that is out of place.

And the evil that we run into in our life does not consist of getting rid of [the particular evil], it is a question of re-adjusting the balance and *keeping* whatever it is that is out of order.[4]

Isaac of Stella, and indeed the desert mystics, understood that all that we project outside of ourselves can be found within. This is described by using the story of Adam and Eve and the serpent (a story that was used earlier in the discussion about shame), in other words there is within us *all* of the elements of paradise – we are each of us Adam, *and* Eve *and* the serpent. The three parts can be roughly seen as firstly the flesh or the body, all the parts of us that are stirred by the senses – this is the serpent. Eve represents the emotional, the aesthetic and the feeling part of each one of us, whilst Adam is the intelligence and the spiritual part of us that are under God. Aside from the rather inevitable gender stereotyping, this is an interesting schema which allows acceptance of every part of the person, rather than denigrating the one and elevating the other – all three are interwoven, and depend on each other, and each is in turn "bad" when it takes over banishing the other aspects. If any one part is exiled then the person is out of balance and divided within him or herself, and unable as a whole person to be in full relationship with God. Merton thought that we are given a few instances in our lives when we have a glimpse of what it is like to balance all these differences, and so know the experience of being integrated. This is "life in all its fullness" (John 10:10).

Merton, in this context, was writing about monastic life, but this objective applies to each of us out in the world. Carl

Jung would have called this objective "individuation." This is an achievement of self-actualisation, where the divisions and the conflict between the conscious and the unconscious become integrated. For Jung this was predominantly about the integration of the shadow into consciousness, and a movement of integration towards becoming oneself, the person one was intended to be and so achieving one's potential. Central to this is the integration of the parts of oneself that are seen as negative and repugnant. Jung understood that this was painful, especially when it requires withdrawing projections onto other people and accepting the rejected and yet unlived aspects of oneself. For Jung, this realization of the self was the goal of life and of being a more complete living being, and interestingly he did not restrict this to human animals as he included everything living. For Jung, the archetype of the self in us was the image of God that then includes the transcendent. He wrote, "Individuation is a transcendent goal, an incarnation."[5]

For both Merton and Jung, overcoming of the divisions gives an increasingly unified grasp of who we are and our own identity. This is purity of heart in the sense of authenticity, openness and clarity, where we discover and accept ourselves. Here acceptance is not a passive action, but rather standing before God naked and defenseless; we are no longer relying on explanations or theories, but rather turning in our vulnerability to God for his grace and his mercy, held in the light of faith. Such openness and vulnerability in the presence of God need not be a sad or dispiriting experience, but rather a relief and joyful as we are then in direct contact with the source of all life. The ultimate realization brought by purity of heart is that our very being is permeated and penetrated by God's love, and knowledge of us, and the more we are known by God the more we find our real identity and being. Correspondingly, there is also the epiphany that the whole of life, and all living beings are permeated by love and life – this may only last for a moment but once experienced not forgotten. Interestingly it was Frank who shared his experience of this with me.

Frank

The other thing I wanted to tell you was that a few months ago, I had this strange and in many ways extraordinary experience. I was sitting in this very ordinary café. It is in the entrance to a shopping mall so not at all beautiful or special but I was sitting there thinking I've no idea what about, and waiting for my coffee to cool down, when it seemed as if the whole place was bathed in what I thought after was a heavenly light. How can I describe it? Well the very tables – only ordinary, and ordinary chairs, seemed very clear and brightly colored, almost as if the very furniture was alive, and the people were oddly beautiful, talking or reading, some on laptops but each one seemed utterly there and real and present in some way. There was a gentle murmur of life, but it also felt vivid. And I felt I was included in it, somehow I was part of it, and I was connected to each of them, it was a wonderful feeling. What is it the politicians say: "we're all in it together," I just felt there was a deep connection between each of us in that place.

I thought about it all the rest of the day, and felt the warmth of some connection with the world which has just been missing. What it made me think was that I was in the end just the same as everyone else, I'm ordinary ... I have my ups and downs, my disappointments and my joys, and this is in the end what life is about. Somehow it was as if I had been affronted by what happened to me, and, yes, perhaps some self-pity, as if I were above the general rule of things. I was expecting, because of my religion and belief in God, that in some ways I was special and so bad things – like Leo's accident – wouldn't happen to me. I thought God had chosen me, and when it went wrong I did see it was my

fault, but it also felt unfair. Something happened in that café, where I felt as if I had a split-second glimpse of what being human really is, as if I got to the heart of it. We're all part of something bigger than ourselves, everybody is, and from what I experienced everything is also connected up. It's all so much more amazing than we allow it to be.

Thomas Merton[6] describes "the heart of it" using the phrase "le point vierge" – literally translated "'the virgin point," which is another way of speaking about an experience of God that affects us in the deepest part of our self. Getting to this experience is a gift aided by contemplation. Merton uses the phrase in his description of an epiphany (not unlike Frank's), that took place ironically outside the confines of his quiet monastery the Abbey of Gethsemani, but instead at the unlikely busy interchange of two streets Fourth and Walnut in the business district of Louisville in Kentucky.

It was as if I suddenly saw the secret beauty of their hearts, the depths of their hearts where neither sin nor desire nor self-knowledge can reach, the core of their reality, the person that each one is in God's eyes ... Again, that expression, le point vierge (I cannot translate it) comes in here. At the center of our being is a point of nothingness which is untouched by sin and by illusion, a point of pure truth, a point or spark which belongs entirely to God, which is never at our disposal ... This little point of nothingness and of absolute poverty is the pure glory of God in us. It is so to speak His name written in us, as our poverty, as our indigence, as our dependence, as our sonship. It is like a pure diamond, blazing with the invisible light of heaven.

The account is of his deep sense of interconnectedness with all the people there, and with the world, and as Jim Forest notes

"This awakening marked the opening of a greater compassion within Merton ... and a deeper sense of connection with the world and its people ... "[7] Here Merton is describing connection as at the very heart of the self and also the heart of faith.

He took the phrase "le point vierge" from the work of Louis Massignon, a Catholic scholar of Islam, where the term has roots in the mystical psychology of Islam as explained in the thought of al-Hallaj, a Sufi mystic and dervish wanderer who died in 922 CE. Al-Hallaj described his experiences of God in this way:

I saw my Lord with the Eye of my heart, and I said: Truly there is no doubt that it is You. It is You that I see in everything; and I do not see You through anything (but You).

He also said that, "our hearts are a virgin that God's truth alone opens"[8] Here "the virgin" is the innermost secret heart of the person; Carl Jung might call it the deep unconscious. But it is here in the very depths of our being, our heart of hearts, in the true self, where the person knows God. Massignon describes the psychology of the Sufi mystic al-Hallaj in this way: "the heart is the organ prepared by God for contemplation. The function cannot be exercised without the organ." As each successive layer is taken away, it is not that with each successive layer the heart disappears, but rather what is happening is mystical union and this is the "sanctifying resurrection" of the heart.

The final covering of the heart ... is the latent personality, the implicit consciousness, the deep subconscious, the secret cell walled up and hidden to every creature, the "inviolate virgin." The latent personality ... remains unformed until God visits ... "[9]

The purified heart is le point vierge the last, irreducible, secret center of the heart; and it is essentially the point of resurrection.

Massignon in a letter to his fellow contemplative and spiritual friend Mary Kahil wrote:

> The return to our origin, to the beginning of our adoption – by re-entering our Mother's womb, as our Lord told Nicodemus, to be born again – by finding again at the bottom of our heart, the virgin point (le point vierge) of our election to Christianity and the action of God's will in us.

He called this mysticism, "the science of hearts" and sees the gradual stripping of the layers as the ridding of errors of judgment and hypocrisies and mental pretences.

> The "heart" designates the incessant oscillation of the human will which beats like the pulse under the impulse of various passions, an impulse which must be stabilized by the Essential Desire, one single God. Introspection must guide us to tear through the concentric "veils" which ensheathe the heart, and hide from us the virginal point (le point vierge) ... wherein God manifests Himself.

Purity of heart is not restricted to our own species. Rather, if we attend to it, we can see that it is the essence and the heart of creation as well. Helen recently told me of a deep experience of connection with all living things as she sat resting in the garden one afternoon.

Helen

It was autumn but one of those mild sunny days and I found myself absorbed by an area of moss which was beside me on the wall. I was very close to it and had never seen it before, but suddenly it was as if I was almost in it, well alongside it at any rate, and rather than just dismissing it as I must have done for years before, I could see that it was a tiny forest. I became very involved, I suppose attentive to it, and although I know nothing about moss I could see there were different sorts depending on where they were on the wall and nearby path – different sizes – all tiny and different shades of green. I forgot how tired I was and just looked and looked – it was as if I couldn't get enough of it. It was like a lost world that I had suddenly found, and I loved it, and I realized that it was alive and in the world just as I am. And yet I'd never given it a moment's thought. It was silent, and yet somehow, if it doesn't sound too silly, the moss spoke to me that day and now whenever I go out there I spend time with the moss.

I told Roger about it and he was looking up moss on the Internet – so we've both got interested, and he found some lines from a poem called "The Moss Method" (Pattiann Rogers) and it's all about how moss despite being so inconspicuous and if you like lowly, still has an effect by powerfully softening sharp edges, rocks and stones and, I can agree with this, I think it's softened the sharp areas of resentment I've had about my illness, and well there's just so much pleasure to be found in it. The final verse of the poem has the lines about clumps of moss that go something like this: "I believe they could comfort the world/with their ministries. That is my hope/even though this world be a jagged rock ..." and it goes on – so beautiful. But it made me feel as if everything is connected, it was a moment of real awareness about the whole world and me in it, and somehow it's helped me see myself, no matter how insignificant and now so limited following the illness – but I'm still part of everything. I also think if God's creation includes such small and insignificant beauty there's hope for us all. I felt I had somehow, and by such a strange route, found myself at the heart of creation!

Helen's epiphany was another form of purification, it was a cleansing and redeeming; the experience was of more than her situation and of a truth that went beyond the superficial. Our hearts are purified through becoming open and vulnerable, through stripping away all the false stuff both in our own hearts and all that surrounds us. This can happen in several ways. We can be affected through the hearts of other people; we are influenced and opened by our experiences of others either directly or through books; through others who have met God, and can describe what has happened to them. Or the experience may just arrive as a gift, as a grace from God. In the final chapter we look at how purity of heart can be helped by prayers of the heart.

Chapter 10

Prayers of the Heart

By "prayer of the heart" we seek God himself present in the depths of our being and meet him there by invoking the name of Jesus in faith, wonder and love.[1]

Just as God mysteriously gave life to our personal being when we knew nothing of it, so now God shapes and forms our inner life in the depths of our hearts, working silently to transform and sometimes to radically reshape us, to conform to God's own likeness.[2]

This final chapter is about prayer. Any authentic prayer is always an impulse of the heart, but this chapter is not about intercessionary prayer in times of joy, fear or need, but instead about wordless prayers of the heart that come from a place of inner quiet and solitude. Such prayer is not a turning away from the corporate church context or of the life of the world, but, rather paradoxically, it is a deepening of involvement in all aspects of life and all of creation. The prayers of the heart are personal, and a way of entering further into the mystery of God. As has been said, it is not enough to have left Egypt, in the sense of following God and having faith in God, but we are invited to enter the Promised Land and with our hearts not just our feet. This is the way towards the inner shrine, toward the consuming fire, toward the presence of God.

All four of our fellow seekers: Carly, Frank, Helen and Stuart, found ways of praying that complemented any collective worship they attended, and took them beyond the usual liturgy into quiet reflective spaces. For Helen, the place of silence took place in her room or in the garden; Stuart and Carly joined meditation groups: Carly, a Christian meditation group where she followed the Jesus prayer, and Stuart, a Zen Christian group where he chanted the heart sutra, whilst Frank went to a Julian group attached to the Cathedral he was attending. Each of them spoke to me about their experiences.

Helen

The more I've had time alone, the more I've felt how necessary it is for me to be quiet and apart. I used to think it was about going away somewhere like a convent, but I've found it right here, it's what I'm calling my inner cave, it's the cave of my heart and I've discovered it doesn't matter where I am as long as I am being attentive and aware. I read this book where the writer says it is about: "a listening for the pulse, the heartbeat, of God within the heart of the world."[3] I never asked for all the extra solitude I've experienced with my illness, but, especially when I can't sleep, I do feel deeply alone except that over time what I've found is that I'm not alone, because I think I have been encountering God, a God who is silent but who then somehow feels as if he is alongside me. The vicar told me there's an expression "alone with the Alone" and that's where I am for the time being. When I was first ill and could no longer do what I'd been used to doing, all that busyness and so on, I felt totally resentful, and my mind was full of how to recover quickly and get back to where I was, so, when I discovered over time that my energy levels were never going to be the same again and my life had to change, I felt very low and actually quite angry, as I thought I've still got a lot to give, and I want to be involved with the family and Roger and the social life I used to have and all that, so I fought against what was the reality, and I'm afraid that didn't help me at all. And I was praying to get better and be healed, and I felt that those prayers were ignored. So my mind was full of grievances and upset and anger, but gradually, and the vicar really helped me, I've found the most healing thing has been to let some of that go on the basis that there's absolutely nothing that I can do, they are just thoughts, so, instead, I set some time aside each day and try to stop thinking about myself and instead to remember God, and think about God, or to try and give God my attention rather than just ask for things. Sometimes I say, "here I am, let it be with me according to thy word," and funnily enough over time this has made me feel better, less agitated and more accepting of the things that I can't change ... Now I see it as a waiting for God and now I think God is waiting for me too. Now I look forward to the time of being alone and as sort of resting with God – just being, and not doing anything else except being there.

My last meeting with Frank was also interesting in that he was still going to services at the Cathedral where he could be one among many, but he told me that he had been attending a fortnightly meeting of a Julian group which met in the town where he now works.

Frank
Well, I saw the notice up in the Cathedral and it so happened that it fitted in with my lunch hour, and I wandered along one time – it's held in this funny little retreat house which I didn't even know existed before. It's just down a side street, and there's an ordinary-sized room with some chairs, and basically you more or less just sit there, in silence for about half an hour and I found it so peaceful. It's very simple – they tell you to stay single-pointed – well focused. We just meet – no one leads it, and so there's no stress about who's in charge and all that, you can just turn up so I try and go, but if I can't I don't feel terrible about it. At the max there's only about six or seven of us, and you don't have to relate, or explain, or justify yourself in any way. In fact it is Christian,

but it doesn't matter what church you belong to. What you do is contemplative prayer or I suppose you can also call it meditation, and I laughed when I read a description of it which says that contemplation or contemplative prayer is where the person concentrates more and more upon less and less.

I try to calm my mind down and stop thinking, and I do feel refreshed after and ready to go back to work – into the fray again. I don't always think of God because I don't really know now what that means, but I do try to clear my mind a bit. I sometimes let thoughts come up and have a look at them, and then try not to get caught up in them too much. If something big comes into my head, I try to shelve it, and think I'll come back to that later. It's like sitting along the river bank and seeing all this stuff floating by in the river – some big logs, but mostly just a lot of debris. Quite honestly, when I do get caught up in thoughts most of it is such rubbish anyway! It helps me understand myself as well, and let go of some of what I used to see as so important. One of the quotes I've found about it is the Matthew 6: 6 verse about, "when you pray, go into your room, close the door and pray to your Father, who is unseen." I like that one, and then only last week I found a quote from a desert father called Abba Moses which goes something like this: "Go, sit in your cell and your cell will teach you everything," and he was writing in the fourth century so this is real wisdom – which I can certainly do with. No, I like the idea that you get wise through being apart and having this time, and that somehow things start to change. Anyway I'm calling it an experiment at present, and I don't yet know how long I'll continue, but it's certainly good having something every couple of weeks.

Both Stuart and Carly decided to go to meditation groups so they could find space and time with God, but in the company of others.

Carly

As you know I was looking for some sense of structure as well as healing, and I thought that being with others would also help. What I like is the regular commitment of meeting once a week, and also there is the time after when we talk a bit over a tea or coffee, but that's usually quite low-key compared to the silence. There's something about being with a group of people (and they're luckily all okay, in fact I feel they're friends!) the feeling is one of connection, and it can feel very powerful too. I've chopped and changed a bit about how I meditate. At the beginning I was following my breath, but then the next minute I was thinking of all my troubles, or the shopping list, so it all got muddled up. One minute something heavy and the next minute something completely irrelevant. We did all talk after one meeting about using a phrase or a word. Some people said they used the word "love" or "peace," but I thought that on the whole I was too muddled for that – as you know I've not felt very loving, and, for a long time – though it's getting better – not at all peaceful. In the end, I found it helpful to say what I needed to say which was, "Oh God, help me" ... and that mostly works for me. If I breathe along with it, and focus on the phrase then I can sometimes have a few minutes where I forget myself and am, I think, just for that moment present to God with my whole heart. A few months ago one of the group was talking about the "Jesus prayer," he also called it "the prayer of the heart" so I'm now trying that – which also works with the breath too. It's an easy prayer and quite simple, and if I get distracted I just start again with it and keep going back to it, and because it fits with the breath it feels natural.

One of the earliest descriptions of the Jesus prayer comes from

St Macarius the Great, who used the phrase from Psalm 19: 14, "The meditation of my heart" to describe a prayer of invoking the name of Christ with deep attention. This he thought was the perfect meditation said in the very ground of one's being – in other words, in the heart seen as the root and source of one's inner truth. St Macarius said:

> There is no other perfect meditation than the saving and blessed Name of Our Lord Jesus Christ dwelling without interruption in you, as it is written "I will cry out like the swallow and I will meditate like the turtledove!" This is what is done by the devout [person] who perseveres in invoking the saving Name of Our Lord Jesus Christ.[4]

The prayer of the heart or the Jesus prayer is simply: "Lord Jesus Christ, Son of God, have mercy on me a sinner." The prayer can be said in various shortened versions, such as "Lord Jesus Christ, have mercy on me," or simply, "Lord Jesus Christ" or "Jesus." Known as the hesychast technique of prayer, it takes us to the ground of our being. Merton wrote that if we are going to find something in ourselves then we have to begin by finding our heart, so as we begin to recite we become conscious of our heart as the center of our being, and as we breathe in we think of the breath going down to our heart, and then it is tied in with the words of the prayer. Repeating the words opens up the heart further, and keeps us held in the center of our deepest identity with and in God. The idea is that the prayer takes root in us – in our hearts so that it becomes a resource for us beyond specific times of prayer.

Those who have practiced this form of prayer tell us that over time our heart can become illumined by a deep confidence, and so transformed by grace. But it is also necessary that then opened through the prayer not only to God but also to our self, we learn to accept our weakness and frailty with a spirit of genuine humility. Making the prayer of the heart our own essentially arises from a state of broken-heartedness, where recognizing our mixed up nature – our love and our hate – we humbly accept our trials, and our true self, and our need of God. It is said that only when we place ourselves in God's love that the Jesus prayer becomes the true prayer of the heart. This can of course be said silently alone, or like Carly silently but within a group.

Stuart had also joined a group – in fact he had been to several including a couple of courses on mindfulness, and had then moved to something a bit different – a group where both Zen Buddhists and Christians met to meditate. When I spoke to Stuart about his meditation group; he also told me about a different prayer of the heart called the heart sutra.

Stuart

As I think I told you last time we spoke, I had begun attending a mindfulness course and going to a group, but since then I've settled, for the time being anyway, with a Buddhist/ Christian group – a set-up where we meet once a fortnight to meditate together. There's a couple of Christians there, and I feel that the practice is really more important for me than worrying about whether I belong to a particular group or not, or for that matter what I identify as. In fact, it's really about going beyond self-image and also belief systems. I also now meditate most days for about twenty minutes at home. I have to say I find it very helpful. Always, at some point, we chant something called "the heart sutra" which in essence is about everything being emptiness, in the sense that it's an illusion. When I first heard it I thought it was crazy, well it makes no sense, especially in the middle part where it goes no this and no that. But I think at another level reciting it breaks up my usual way of thinking about things, and it's not just about beliefs, but about the way I now see the world and who I am in it, yes even at this advanced stage of my life! Actually it's been a bit of breakthrough after all that searching. Anyway, it's called the heart sutra because it conveys what they call the heart essence of wisdom or insight, and you can also contemplate or meditate on it.

The lines I like especially are: "form does not differ from emptiness; emptiness does not differ from form. Form itself is emptiness; emptiness itself is form. So too are feeling, cognition, formation, and consciousness." You can see things just get canceled out, and then you see that things are not what they seem, including me, they are more like illusions or even dreams. The paradox of the whole thing as you are searching, like I was to find God and make sense of it all, especially at this stage of my life, is, I think, to get to a place where you stop searching and seeking, and trying to grasp, and hold onto a belief that sees you through everything. Someone said, well, what happens when there is no place left to go with our thinking? It's not that if something is not something then it is nothing ... that's the whole thing about either/or rather it can be both/and.

So, from what I can understand about it even though everything is emptiness it is still compassion. I think it's said that at the heart of emptiness there is compassion. So, it's very strange, and part of that compassion is practicing something called loving kindness towards ourselves and the world – well, in fact, the whole of creation. So that's where I am at present. When I talk about it with my wife, I think I don't particularly understand it, but in a strange way it also helps me make sense of everything – it helps me see things as they are, and not to be overly attached to one thing or another. And it doesn't stop me sometimes going to church with her – especially to holy communion where I think I now accept that everything is part of the mystery, and everything connects one way or another, and, amazingly I don't have to understand it all either!

Speaking to Stuart reminded me of the famous account of Thomas Merton's epiphany, a few days before he died in 1968, in front of the huge statues of the Buddha in Polonnaruwa in what is now Sri Lanka.[5]

> Looking at those figures I was suddenly, almost forcibly, jerked clean out of the habitual, half-tied vision of things, and an inner clearness, clarity, as if exploding from the rocks themselves, became evident and obvious. The queer evidence of the reclining figure, the smile, the sad smile of Ananda standing with arms folded ... The thing about all this is that there is no puzzle, no problem, and really no "mystery." All problems are resolved and everything is clear, simply because what matters is clear. The rock, all matter, all life is charged with *dharmakaya* – everything is emptiness and everything is compassion. I don't know when in my life I have ever had such a sense of beauty and spiritual validity running together in one aesthetic illumination ... I mean, I know and have seen what I was obscurely looking for. I don't know what else remains but I have now seen and have pierced through the surface and got beyond the shadow and the disguise.

Spiritual searching leads each one of us to strange places, but inevitably and truthfully always back towards the heart of our self and our interior life. The paradox is that no matter where we seek God in external structures, he is to be found right where we started from within each heart – both transcendent and immanent. He is, as we search, both familiar and also utterly unknown, both near and at times far, consistent and unpredictable – God.

> Have you found what you sought, my soul? You sought God, and you found God to be the highest of all things, than which nothing better could be conceived; you found God to be Life

itself and Light, Wisdom and Good, eternal Blessedness and blessed Eternity; you found God to be everywhere and always.[6]

You found God in your heart of hearts.

References

Epigraph

1. Alexander Ryrie, (2012) *The Prayer of Silence*, Oxford, SLG Press, 2012, 23

Preface

1. Thomas Merton, (1998) *The Other Side of the Mountain, The Journals of Thomas Merton*, vol. 7, HarperSanFrancisco, 323

Introduction

1. Thomas Merton, (1973) *Contemplative Prayer*, London, Darton, Longman and Todd, 22
2. This quotation and the subsequent quotations in this section are all taken from Andrew Harvey, (1998) *Son of Man, The Mystical Path to Christ*, New York, Jeremy P. Tarcher/Putnam, 206–7

Chapter 1 Hungry Hearts – Seeking God in the Wilderness

1. Nicolas Berdyaev, (1943) *Slavery and Freedom*, London, Geoffrey Bles, The Centenary Press, 16
2. H. A. Williams, (1965) *The True Wilderness*, London, Constable, 30
3. Thomas Merton, (1948) *The Seven Storey Mountain*. New York, Harcourt, Brace, 201
4. Williams, (1965) *True Wilderness*, 27–8
5. Etty Hillesum, (1999) *An Interrupted Life, The Diaries and Letters of Etty Hillesum, 1941–1943*, London, Persephone Books, 23–4
6. William H. Shannon, (2002) 'God' in *The Thomas Merton Encyclopedia*, (ed) William H. Shannon, et al., Maryknoll, New York, Orbis, 182
7. William Blake, (1966) 'The Marriage of Heaven and Hell', *The Complete Writings of William Blake*, (ed) by Geoffrey

Keynes, London, Oxford University Press, pp. 148–158, 154

8. C. G. Jung, (1932) *Psychology and Religion: West and East*, London and Henley, Routledge and Kegan Paul, 330, par.497

9. William Johnston, (2000) *Arise, My Love, Mysticism for a New Era*, Maryknoll, New York: Orbis, 29

10. Bernard Lonergan, (1974) *A Second Collection*, London, Darton, Longman and Todd, 4, 63

Chapter 2 Disheartened, and with Hardened Hearts

1. Ideas about the development of the false and compliant self are found in D. W. Winnicott, (1982) *The Maturational Processes and the Facilitating Environment*, London, Hogarth Press and the Institute of Psycho-Analysis

2. Dorothee Soelle, (1975) *Suffering*, Philadelphia, Fortress Press, 38

Chapter 3 A Heart of Flesh – Being Human

1. Thomas Merton, (1973) *Contemplative Prayer*, 25

2. C. G. Jung, (1973) *Letters*, vol.1, London, Routledge and Kegan Paul, 33

3. Carlos G. Valles, (1992) *I Love You I Hate You*, London, Darton, Longman and Todd, 22

4. Rev James Martin, SJ, (30.3.2011) 'How to Love your enemies', https://www.huffpost.com/author/rev-james-martin-sj (Accessed 4 November 2019)

Chapter 4 A Contrite Heart

1. H. A. Williams, (1965), *True Wilderness*, 83

2. Richard Coles, (2014) *Fathomless Riches*, London, Weidenfeld and Nicolson, 254

3. Thomas Merton, (1948) *Seven Storey Mountain*, 193

4. John Jacob Raub, *Who Told You That You Were Naked*, New York, Crossroad, 1993, 97

5. H. A. Williams, (1982) *Some Day I'll Find You*, London,

Mitchell Beazley, 45, 93

6. Dennis McCort, (2017) *A Kafkaesque Memoir*, Berlin, Palm Art Press, 261

7. C. G. Jung, (1976) *Letters,* vol. 2, London, Routledge and Kegan Paul, 367–370

8. William H. Shannon, (2002) 'Sin', *The Thomas Merton Encyclopedia*, 439

9. Carlos G. Valles, (1992) *I Love You I Hate You*, London, Darton, Longman and Todd, 95

10. H. A. Williams, (1965) *True Wilderness*, 100

11. Thomas Merton, (1977) *The Collected Poems of Thomas* Merton, New York, New Directions Book, 449

Chapter 5 Broken-Hearted

1. H. A. Williams, (1984) *True to Experience*, an anthology (ed) Eileen Mable, London, Mitchell Beazley, 123

2. William Johnston, (1993) *The Mystical Way*, London, Fount HarperCollins, 262

3. Thomas Merton, (1996) *Entering the Silence, The Journals of Thomas Merton,* vol. 2, (ed) Jonathon Montaldo, New York, HarperCollins, 382–384

4. Thomas Merton, (1997) *A Search for Solitude, The Journals of Thomas Merton,* vol. 3, (ed) Lawrence S. Cunningham, New York, HarperCollins, 22

5. Merton, (1997) *A Search for Solitude*, 23, 25, 27

6. Williams, (1982) *Some Day I'll Find You*, 167–177

7. Raub, (1993) *Who Told You*, 86

8. Williams, (1965) *True Wilderness*, 84

9. Thomas Merton, (1974) *A Thomas Merton Reader*, (ed) Thomas P. McDonnell, New York and London, Doubleday, 351

10. Merton, (1974), *Thomas Merton Reader*, 355–6

11. Williams, (1965) *True Wilderness*, 84

12. Williams, (1984) *True to Experience*, 123

Chapter 6 Two Halves and One Heart

1. Aleksandr Solzhenitsyn, (1974) *The Gulag Archipelago,* London and New York, Collins, 17
2. Williams, (1984) *True to Experience,* 137
3. Iain Matthew, (1995) *The Impact of God,* London, Hodder and Stoughton
4. Matthew, (1995) *The Impact of God,* 69
5. Matthew, (1995) *The Impact of God,* 78
6. Matthew, (1995) *The Impact of God,* 90
7. C. G. Jung, (1958) *Psychology and Religion: West and East, The Collected Works of C. G. Jung* vol. 11, London and Henley, Routledge & Kegan Paul, 340, par. 522. See also C. G. Jung, (1953) *Psychology and Alchemy, The Collected Works of C. G. Jung* vol.12 Bollingen Series XX Princeton, N.J., Princeton University Press, 186, par 259
8. H. Lawrence Bond, (1997) *Nicholas of Cusa, Selected Spiritual Writings* New York, Mahwah, Paulist Press, 252–3
9. Bond, (1997) *Nicholas of Cusa,* 20 and 261
10. Thomas Merton, (1995) *Conjectures of a Guilty Bystander,* Tunbridge Wells, Kent, Burns and Oates, 21
11. Thomas Merton, (1961) "Herakleitos the Obscure" in *The Behavior of Titans,* New York, New Directions, 82

Chapter 7 Taking Heart

1. Albert Camus, (1968) 'Return to Tipasa', *Lyrical and Critical Essays,* New York, Vintage, 162–172, 169
2. Donald J. Goergen, O.P. (2002) 'Globalization of Hope', http://opcentral.org/blog/globalization-of-hope/ (Accessed 4 November2019)
3. Leo Tolstoy, (1981) *The Death of Ivan Ilyich,* New York, Bantam Books, 132
4. Helen's two readings are taken from *Precious Thoughts, Daily Readings from the Correspondence of Thomas Merton,* (2004) (ed) Fiona Gardner, London, Darton, Longman and Todd,

53–54

5. James Alison, (2003) 'Contemplation in a World of Violence II, The Strangeness of this Passivity,' *The Merton Journal*, 4–12, 4
6. Matthew, (1995) *The Impact of God*, 95–101
7. Jim Forest, (2014) 'Thomas Merton as a Messenger of Hope', in *We Are Already One*, (eds) Gray Henry and Jonathan Montaldo, Louisville, KY, Fons Vitae, 30–34, 33
8. Alison, (2003) 'Contemplation in a World of Violence', 5
9. Chris MacKenna, (2005) 'The Experience of Transformation', presentation at Sarum College, unpublished, 1–6, 3
10. Thomas Merton, (1998) *The Other Side of the Mountain*, 113
11. Sebastian Moore, (2003) 'Peace in a Time of Terror', *The Merton Journal*, 14–26, 23
12. Fiona Gardner, (2015) *The Only Mind Worth Having, Thomas Merton and the Child Mind*, Eugene, Oregon, Cascade
13. Moore, (2003) 'Peace in a Time of Terror', 25
14. Alison, (2003) 'Contemplation in a World of Violence', 11
15. C. G. Jung, (1961) *Memories, Dreams and Reflections*, London, Collins Fount, 18
16. Alison, (2003) 'Contemplation in a World of Violence', 9–10

Chapter 8 A Change of Heart

1. Neville Symington, (2001) *The Spirit of Sanity*, London, Karnac Press
2. Bernard Lonergan, (1972) *Method in Theology*, New York, Herder and Herder, cited in W. Conn, (1986) *Christian Conversion*, Mahwah, New Jersey, Paulist Press, 27
3. Thomas Merton, (1953) *The Sign of Jonas*, London, Hollis and Carter, 149
4. Thomas Merton, (1975) *He Is Risen*, Niles, IL, Argus Communications, 26–27, 42
5. Rowan Williams, (1982) *Resurrection*, London, Darton Longman and Todd, 29

6. These ideas and the quotations in this paragraph are taken from Thomas Merton, (1989) *'Honourable Reader': Reflections on My Work*, (ed) Robert E. Daggy, New York, Crossroad, 143–151

Chapter 9 Getting to the Heart of It

1. Roberta E. Bondi, (1995) *Memories of God*, London, Darton, Longman and Todd, 171, 173
2. Julian of Norwich, (1987) *Revelations of Divine Love*, London, Hodder and Stoughton
3. Thomas Merton, (1988) *The Wisdom of the Desert*, London, Darley Anderson, 8
4. Thomas Merton, (2010) 'A Conference on Integration: Praying from the Heart' (ed) David M. Odorisio, *Merton Seasonal*, vol. 35, no.1, 28–33, 29
5. C. G. Jung, (1976) *Letters*, vol.2, 14
6. Thomas Merton, (1995) *Conjectures of a Guilty Bystander*, 156–158
7. Jim Forest, (2016) *The Root of War Is Fear, Thomas Merton's Advice to Peacemakers*, Maryknoll, New York, Orbis Books, 18
8. Christine M. Bochen, (2002) 'Le point vierge' in *The Thomas Merton Encyclopedia*, 363
9. Sidney H. Griffiths, 'Thomas Merton, Louis Massignon, and the Challenge of Islam', in *The Merton Annual*, vol. 3, 151–172

Chapter 10 Prayers of the Heart

1. Thomas Merton, (1973) *Contemplative Prayer*, 34
2. Alexander Ryrie, (2012) *The Prayer of Silence*, 24
3, Donald Eadie, foreword to Alexander Ryrie, (2012) *The Prayer of Silence*, iii.
4, Merton, (1973) *Contemplative Prayer*, 22
5. Thomas Merton, (1998) *The Other Side of the Mountain*, 321–323

6. *The Proslogion by St Anselm of Canterbury* (2015) in Benedictine Daily Prayer, Collegeville, Minnesota, Liturgical Press, 1749

Scripture quotations are from the *New Revised Standard Version* (Oxford University Press 1995)

THE NEW OPEN SPACES

Throughout the two thousand years of Christian tradition there
have been, and still are, groups and individuals that exist in
the margins and upon the edge of faith. But in Christianity's
contrapuntal history it has often been these outcasts and
pioneers that have forged contemporary orthodoxy out
of former radicalism as belief evolves to engage with and
encompass the ever-changing social and scientific realities. Real
faith lies not in the comfortable certainties of the Orthodox,
but somewhere in a half-glimpsed hinterland on the dirt track
to Emmaus, where the Death of God meets the Resurrection,
where the supernatural Christ meets the historical Jesus,
and where the revolution liberates both the oppressed and
the oppressors.

Welcome to Christian Alternative... a space at the edge where
the light shines through.
If you have enjoyed this book, why not tell other readers by
posting a review on your preferred book site.

Recent bestsellers from Christian Alternative are:

Bread Not Stones
The Autobiography of An Eventful Life
Una Kroll
The spiritual autobiography of a truly remarkable woman
and a history of the struggle for ordination in the Church of
England.
Paperback: 978-1-78279-804-0 ebook: 978-1-78279-805-7

The Quaker Way
A Rediscovery
Rex Ambler
Although fairly well known, Quakerism is not well understood.
The purpose of this book is to explain how Quakerism works as
a spiritual practice.
Paperback: 978-1-78099-657-8 ebook: 978-1-78099-658-5

Blue Sky God
The Evolution of Science and Christianity
Don MacGregor
Quantum consciousness, morphic fields and blue-sky
thinking about God and Jesus the Christ.
Paperback: 978-1-84694-937-1 ebook: 978-1-84694-938-8

Celtic Wheel of the Year
Tess Ward
An original and inspiring selection of prayers combining
Christian and Celtic Pagan traditions, and interweaving their
calendars into a single pattern of prayer for every morning
and night of the year.
Paperback: 978-1-90504-795-6

Christian Atheist
Belonging without Believing
Brian Mountford
Christian Atheists don't believe in God but miss him: especially
the transcendent beauty of his music, language, ethics, and
community.
Paperback: 978-1-84694-439-0 ebook: 978-1-84694-929-6

Compassion Or Apocalypse?
A Comprehensible Guide to the Thoughts of René Girard
James Warren
How René Girard changes the way we think about God and the
Bible, and its relevance for our apocalypse-threatened world.
Paperback: 978-1-78279-073-0 ebook: 978-1-78279-072-3

Diary Of A Gay Priest
The Tightrope Walker
Rev. Dr. Malcolm Johnson
Full of anecdotes and amusing stories, but the Church is still a
dangerous place for a gay priest.
Paperback: 978-1-78279-002-0 ebook: 978-1-78099-999-9

Do You Need God?
Exploring Different Paths to Spirituality Even For Atheists
Rory J.Q. Barnes
An unbiased guide to the building blocks of spiritual belief.
Paperback: 978-1-78279-380-9 ebook: 978-1-78279-379-3

Readers of ebooks can buy or view any of these bestsellers by clicking on the live link in the title. Most titles are published in paperback and as an ebook. Paperbacks are available in traditional bookshops. Both print and ebook formats are available online.

Find more titles and sign up to our readers' newsletter at
http://www.johnhuntpublishing.com/christianity
Follow us on Facebook at
https://www.facebook.com/ChristianAlternative